STREETS
AND THE SHAPING
OF TOWNS AND CITIES

STREETS
AND THE SHAPING
OF TOWNS AND CITIES

Michael Southworth

Eran Ben-Joseph

McGraw-Hill

New York • San Francisco • Washington, D.C. • Auckland
Bogotá • Caracas • Lisbon • London • Madrid • Mexico City • Milan
Montreal • New Delhi • San Juan • Singapore • Sydney • Tokyo • Toronto

Library of Congress Cataloging-in-Publication Data

Southworth, Michael.
    Streets and the shaping of towns and cities : Michael Southworth,
Eran Ben-Joseph.
      p.   cm.
    Includes bibliographical references and index.
    ISBN 0-07-059808-8
    1. Streets—Design. 2. City Planning. 3. Streets—Standards.
I. Ben-Joseph, Eran. II. Title.
TE279.S58   1996   96-14939
711'. 7—dc20   CIP

McGraw-Hill

A Division of The *McGraw-Hill* Companies

1 2 3 4 5 6 7 8 9 0 DOC/DOC 9 0 1 0 9 8 7 6

ISBN 0-07-059808-8

The sponsoring editor for this book was *Wendy Lochner,*
the editing supervisor was *Bernard Onken,*
and the production supervisor was *Suzanne W. B. Rapcavage.*
It was designed and set in Sabon by *TopDesk Publishers' Group.*

Printed and bound by *R.R. Donnelley & Sons Company.*

McGraw-Hill books are available at special quantity discounts to use as premiums
and sales promotions, or for use in corporate training programs. For more information, please write to the Director of Special Sales, McGraw-Hill, 11 West 19th
Street, New York, NY 10011. Or contact your local bookstore.

This book is printed on acid-free paper.

Contents

Acknowledgments

We are grateful for research grants and other assistance from the Institute of Transportation Studies, the Institute of Urban and Regional Development, the University of California Transportation Center, the Committee on Research, and the Farrand Fund of the University of California at Berkeley. Ray Isaacs, Mathew Henning, and Adrienne Wong provided graphic assistance in several of the original maps. Portions of this book are related to research by the authors published as articles in the *Journal of the American Planning Association* and working papers by the Institute of Urban and Regional Development and the Institute of Transportation Studies.

Introduction

Street Standards and the Built Environment

There has been a decided tendency on the part of official street planners to insist with quite needless and undesirable rigidity upon certain fixed standards of width and arrangement in regard to purely local streets, leading inevitably in many cases to the formation of blocks and lots of a size and shape ill adapted to the local uses to which they need to be put.

—Frederick Law Olmsted, 1910

Frederick Law Olmsted's critique of street standards more than eight decades ago is, surprisingly, even more relevant today as cities worldwide grow at an unprecedented rate. Most of this growth, as in centuries past, is at the edges of older towns and cities on open land that until recently was used for agriculture, or simply left as natural open space. Cities have always grown at their edges, with new residential quarters taking root on established urban nodes. Suburban enclaves and rural villages that once seemed to be at the outer limits of urbanity, over time often have found themselves swept into the

Today cities like Los Angeles have absorbed rural villages, towns, and suburbs in the rush of outward expansion. *(© William Garnett)*

inner metropolis. London, a classic example of such growth, is today an agglomeration of independent towns, suburbs, and rural villages that were caught in this net of outward expansion. The same process can be seen in the historical growth patterns of Boston, Los Angeles, the San Francisco Bay area, and indeed of most cities.

Each era of urban expansion has had its own conceptions of the good city, its own processes and standards for city building. A key element in the shaping of cities has been ideas of what the residential street network should be, since streets are the public frameworks within which neighborhood life takes place. What should be the character, pattern, and materials of streets and how should one street relate to another? What activities should the street accommodate? How wide should streets be and how should they be furnished and planted? In less than a century American conceptions of the good residential street network have shifted dramatically from the interconnected rectilinear grid of the turn of the century, to the fragmented grid and warped parallel streets of the 1930s and 1940s, to the discontinuous, insular patterns of cul-de-sacs and loops that have predominated since World War II until the present time.

In this book we examine the origins of ideas for the design of residential streets, focusing on the suburban subdivision. We question the standards that have in large measure created the modern suburban residential environment that comprises so much of the metropolitan area. As not only the fastest growing part of American cities, but also the home for the majority of Americans, areas of new growth would be most affected by changes in street standards.

Rethinking of suburban street standards is needed today to create more cohesive, livable, and energy-efficient communities and metropolitan areas. Yet attempts to do so meet with resistance from many quarters: engineers, financial institutions, government regulators, the road building industry, as well as police and fire protection services all have vested interests in the street regulations as they have evolved. Efforts to reshape the form of the American city are often thwarted by these standards and procedures that have become embedded in planning and development. Particularly troublesome are standards for streets that virtually dictate a dispersed, disconnected community pattern providing automobile access at the expense of other modes. The rigid framework of current

Over the past century American conceptions of the residential street network have changed dramatically from the interconnected rectilinear grid of the turn-of-the-century (a), to the fragmented grid and warped parallel streets of the 1930s and 1940s (b), to the discontinuous, insular patterns of cul-de-sacs and loops that have been preferred since the 1950s. *(© Michael Southworth)*

street standards has resulted in uniform, unresponsive suburban environments that ignore the local situation. Do existing suburban spatial patterns justify adherence to the rationality of standardization? Why did the design process and built environment come to depend on these criteria and regulations? How did residential street standards come to be? Who has been responsible for their formulation? How have they changed over time? These are some of the issues we need to understand and evaluate as a prelude to new consideration of the developing urban environment. There are also subjects we do not address, namely, the design of major arterials, boulevards, highways, and streets in commercial areas, nor streets in the older inner residential neighborhoods of cities, although each of these is important and deserving of a similar investigation.

Street standards may appear benign but are powerful in the way they shape the environments we live in. The public commonly credits—and blames—designers, planners, and developers for the sprawling, monotonous form of suburbia today, assuming they have full control over the quality of the built environment. In fact, the design and building professions must usually work within a framework of controls and standards that specify many aspects of subdivision layout. Simple dimensions for minimum street width, sidewalks, or planting strips may seem innocuous, but when applied to miles of streets in hundreds of subdivisions occupied by millions of people, they have an enormous impact on the way our neighborhoods look, feel, and work for us. For example, a modest change in pavement width can have large consequences for energy consumption, comfort and convenience, sociability, the time and effort we must spend in local trips, as well as the costs of construction and maintenance. Land devoted to the street right-of-way takes away from the area devoted to residential units, thus reducing the size of lots. An increase in street width also increases construction and maintenance costs proportionately, lowers densities (assuming the same lot size and housing type), and increases travel times between points.

This does not mean we should abolish standards. Obviously, design and engineering standards can and often do assure a minimum level of quality and performance, as in many plans and construction standards designed to protect our health and safety. The problem arises when standards intended for health and safety overstep their bounds and lose a grounding in objective measures of goodness or a connection with the original rationale for their existence. We believe this is what has happened with residential street standards today. The residential environment is being shaped in major ways by standards that are no longer questioned and that have become part of a rigid framework that is closed to change.

Through the years, the design and layout of residential streets in the United States has become increasingly regulated. Methodical administration of public works, the centralized supervision over land development beginning in the 1930s, and the rise of the road and transportation engineering professions have established street standards as justifiable absolutes.

THE POWER OF STREET STANDARDS

Simple standards for street width and alignment have an enormous impact on the way neighborhoods look, feel, and work. In the course of the twentieth century, design and layout of residential streets has become increasingly regulated in the United States. *(©William Garnett)*

As car ownership and mobility have grown, engineers have assumed that streets must be enlarged accordingly. The result has been regulations and standards that are often in excess of actual traffic requirements. Design of the residential street network is based on statistical information and research that is primarily oriented to facilitating vehicle movement on large-scale streets and highways. Such standards have then been mechanically adopted and legitimized by local governments to shield themselves from any responsibility for road performance. Federal funds for street improvements have further entrenched uniform standards. Local agencies have been required to adhere to minimum geometrical design criteria in order to be eligible for monetary assistance. Modifications have been discouraged and because higher governmental agencies have not openhandedly allowed flexibility, lesser agencies have been reluctant to do so. Additionally, financial institutions and commercial developers embraced conventional suburban street and parking layouts. Lenders in turn have been hesitant to support a development outside the mainstream, particularly when it did not conform to established standards and regulations. Commercial developers favored segregated land use patterns based on the "drive-park-shop" concept. As a result they required standards specifying wide streets, ample parking, and ease of movement in return for taking on a project.

THE SOCIAL AND ENVIRONMENTAL IMPACTS OF STREET STANDARDS

As designers and planners reassess the physical form of the urban edge there is growing recognition of the physical and social impacts of standardized streets on the environment. Cumulative figures show that, worldwide, at least one third of all developed urban land is devoted to roads, parking lots, and other motor vehicle infrastructure. In the urban United States, the automobile consumes close to half the land area of cities; in Los Angeles the figure approaches two thirds.[1,2] Moreover, much of the built road space is actually wasted considering that local residential streets constitute 80 percent of the total national road miles while they carry only 15 percent of total vehicle miles traveled.[3]

Waste of street space and its economic impact has been a prolonged phenomenon. Since the 1930s, suburban subdivisions have been dominated by single-family residences fronting extensive paved streets. The prevailing right-of-way width for a residential subdivision street, as specified by the Institute of Transportation Engineers, has remained at 50 to 60 feet (15.2–18.3 m) for the last 30 years.[4] Designating this generous space for an exclusive mono-functional land use within a residential environment has created suburban environments that are unnecessarily wasteful of land, energy, and materials.[5] In a typical suburban subdivision with 5000 square-foot (450 sq m) lots and 56-foot (17 m) rights-of-way, streets amount to approximately 30 percent of the total development. When typical 20-foot (6 m) driveway setbacks are included, the total amount of paved space reaches about 50 percent of the development. At present, with the cost of land representing 25 percent of the cost of a single-family house in most of the country (up from

An amazing amount of land is devoted to roads, parking lots, and other vehicular infrastructure in the United States, particularly in post–World War II developments. On the average, the automobile consumes nearly half the land area of cities in the United States, and in some cities like Los Angeles, it approaches two thirds. *(© William Garnett)*

Excessive street standards that require wide streets and large setbacks have major social and economic impacts. They waste land, drive up home costs, and negate the essence of residential livability. The functions of streets have been diminished by the emphasis on motorized accessibility. *(© Eran Ben-Joseph)*

10 percent in the 1950s), one would assume that a shift toward efficient and compact subdivision planning would occur.[6] Yet, street standards as well as land allocated for street use remain excessive.

The extensive allocation of land for circulation purposes in residential suburbia has resulted not only in the depletion of land and an increase in the economic burden for all, but it also has had social consequences. Street codes and standards that were established to facilitate vehicular travel performance have undermined residential livability. The use of streets as settings for social interaction has often been compromised, if not prevented, by the emphasis on motorized accessibility. The Urban Land Institute stresses this point: "It was often forgotten that residential streets become part of the neighborhood and are eventually used for a variety of purposes for which they were not designed. Residential streets provide direct auto access for the occupant to his home; they carry traffic past his home; they provide a visual setting, an entryway for each house; a pedestrian circulation system; a meeting place for residents; a play area (whether one likes it or not) for the children, etc. To design and engineer residential streets solely for the convenience of easy automobile movement overlooks the many overlapping uses of a residential street."[7] The concept of the street as a physical and social part of the house and its surroundings is critical, both to the physical design of the neighborhood and to the design and operating philosophy for the local street system. However, the paradigms of traffic-oriented streets have been directed toward expanding street manageability and traffic capacity.

ABOUT THIS BOOK

As a prelude to reevaluating the suburban environment, we have traced the evolution of suburban residential street standards through a review of professional and technical publications, along with built projects, over the past two centuries in both England and the United States. We have attempted to understand the forces that helped shape each period, as well as its significance for street form today. For each phase in the evolution of standards we have analyzed its conceptual framework, design prototypes, administrative acts, construction techniques, and normative design criteria. Among the most useful sources on the origin of American suburban street standards are government and professional handbooks for subdivision development such as those issued by the Federal Housing Administration, the Housing and Home Finance Agency, the Institute of Transportation Engineers, and the Urban Land Institute. Of particular interest to urban design is Charles Mulford Robinson's 1911 study, *The Width and Arrangement of Streets*. General works on urban history and the development process such as those by Harold Lautner, Walter Creese, Christine Boyer, Robert Fishman, and Marc Weiss have been valuable in tracing the chain of events leading to standardization and in studying street standards in the context of larger processes.

In the next chapters we discuss the major historical shifts in the development of residential street guidelines and standards. During the first period, 1820–1870, we find the origins of modern suburban design standards in the early suburbs of England and the United States inspired by the picturesque movement in design. In the second period, 1870–1930, the chaotic and unhealthful living conditions of the early industrial city spurred legislation

Residential streets serve many functions beyond vehicular access—they are settings for social activity including children's play and adult recreation, the framework for pedestrian and bicycle circulation, and the space that provides an entry to homes. They should be designed for all of these activities. *(a: © Eran Ben-Joseph; b, c, d: © Donald Appleyard)*

for residential street standards. Rigid "bye-law" standards for street design in English cities stimulated a reaction. Designers like Raymond Unwin, Barry Parker, and Norman Shaw tried to avoid such uniformity and emphasized urban design values in their work. During this period, another force had major impacts on the design of streets and neighborhoods, especially in the United States: the rise of the automobile as the main form of transportation. The idea of the neighborhood was reexamined and designers Clarence Stein and Henry Wright introduced new ways of structuring neighborhood space and the street network. At the same time, European Modernist architects like Le Corbusier, Walter Gropius, and Ludwig Hilberseimer borrowed the traffic-protected superblock idea to create "machine-age" cities on a new scale designed expressly for the automobile. In the third period, 1930–1950, residential street standards and the form of the modern suburb in the United States became institutionalized with the establishment of the Federal Housing Administration, which disseminated street design guidelines and standards as part of FHA loan programs. In the fourth period, 1950–1985, transportation engineering developed as a profession and the Institute of Transportation Engineers was founded. Street standards and street design focused almost exclusively on the needs of the motorist. Finally, we conclude with discussions of alternatives to the standards now in place and ways of developing new neighborhood street standards. Today the standards for neighborhood streets that have evolved are being questioned by many designers, planners, and even engineers. Several alternatives are being experimented with that place greater emphasis on the role of the street in the life of neighborhoods. Whether changes can be effected will depend not only upon having a vision of what is possible, but understanding how we have gotten to our present state. Let us hope that by becoming more aware of how street standards have evolved over time and how deeply they affect our living environment, we can work to make them more humane.

Gritty Cities and Picturesque Villages

The Origins of Suburban Street Design Standards in England and the United States

> *The joy and pain of urban existence, the comfort or hardship of it, its efficiency or failure are influenced by the wisdom or the thoughtlessness with which streets are platted.*
>
> —Charles Mulford Robinson, 1911

Today's standards for street design have roots in ancient practice and road building technologies. Roman street standards and paving ordinances provided the foundation for modern road building technique and design. In Mediterranean towns streets were typically narrow and wheeled traffic was controlled, thus eliminating the need for wider streets. Moreover, the hot climate made the shady narrow streets more comfortable. In the first century B.C., the Roman architect and engineer Vitruvius advised that streets should be laid out to control winds, which would bring humidity and disease into the city: "When the walls are set round the city, there follow the divisions of the sites within the walls, and the layings out of the broad streets and the alleys with a view to aspect. These will be rightly laid out if the winds are carefully shut out from the alleys. For if the winds are cold they are unpleasant; if hot, they infect; if moist, they are injurious. . . . For when the quarters of the city are planned to meet the winds full, the rush of air and the frequent breezes from the open space of the sky will move with mightier power, confined as they are in the jaws of the alleys. Wherefore the directions of the streets are to avoid the quarters of the winds, so that when the winds come up against the corners of the blocks of buildings they may be broken, driven back and dissipated."[1] Vitruvius went on at length on the names and characteristics of the different winds and how to lay out the streets accordingly.

The earliest known written law regarding streets dates back to about 100 B.C., and fixed the width of Roman streets at a minimum of 15 feet (4.5 m).[2] Previous street construction did not follow any regulations. In Pompeii until 200 B.C., the streets were paved at various widths while the houses facing them were low and small. When the *peristyle* or courtyard house came into fashion from 200 B.C. to 100 B.C., houses encroached into the street and formed narrower arcade streets similar to those of Hellenistic cities. Romans later adopted this style which reached its peak in the Imperial period. The tendency to build higher houses created dark and narrow passages, insufficient for wheeled traffic. As a result, in 15 B.C. Augustus limited the height of buildings to 66 feet (20 m) and no more than six stories. He also made a new law fixing the main intersecting axes of the grid: the *decumanus*, the

Streets were narrow and paved in ancient Mediterranean towns like Jerusalem. In the hot climate, narrow shady streets were more comfortable for pedestrians, and since wheeled traffic was regulated, there was no need for wide streets. (© Eran Ben-Joseph)

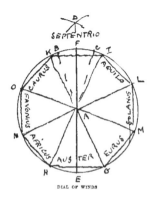

DIAL OF WINDS

PLAN OF TOWN

The Roman architect and engineer Vitruvius wrote on the layout of streets in the first century B.C. He conceived his octagonal ideal city to control the eight winds, which he analyzed in some detail in his treatise on architecture. (Frank Granger)

east–west processional road, was to be 40 feet (12.2 m); the *cardo*, the main north–south road, was set at 20 feet (6 m); and the *vicinae*, side roads, were to be 15 feet (4.5 m).

Streets of Rome were usually paved with basalt slabs. Elevated sidewalks paved with peperino stone were usually built on both sides of the street and

The excavations at Herculaneum, which was buried in lava when Vesuvius erupted in 79 A.D., uncovered a typical Roman city street from the first century A.D. The street is narrow and paved in stone, with raised sidewalks on both sides. Several houses encroach into the street to form protective arcades at the pedestrian level.
(© Alinari/ArtResource, N.Y.)

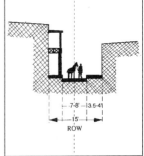

Emperor Augustus set standards for street widths in 15 B.C. The width of *vicinae*—side roads—was about 15 feet. (© Eran Ben-Joseph)

took as much as half of the total street width. Roads outside the city were either paved, or at minimum, graveled. In 47 B.C. traffic congestion became such a problem citywide that Caesar forbade transport during the daytime except for materials for public buildings or for festivals and games. Wagon transport including the removal of refuse and rubble to the dumps outside the towns was restricted to nighttime.

While the Roman city street, with its elevated sidewalks, became the prototype for modern street design, it was *viae militares*, military roads, that were the foundation for contemporary construction techniques. By the peak of the Roman Empire in 300 A.D., almost 53,000 miles of military roads had been built connecting Rome with the frontiers. The typical Roman road was constructed of four layers: flat stones, crushed stones, gravel, and coarse sand mixed with lime. Paving stones and a wearing surface of mortar and a flint-

The Roman *viae militares*, or military roads, like the Appian Way connected Rome with the outer limits of the empire. These roads became the prototype for modern road construction.
(©Donald Appleyard)

like lava were laid on top. Roads were usually about 35 feet (10.6 m) wide, with two central lanes 15.5 (4.7 m) feet wide for two directions of traffic, and were lined by freestanding curbstones 2 feet (.6 m) wide and 18 inches (45 cm) tall. On the outer side of the curbs a one-way lane about 7.5 feet (2.3 m) wide was laid. This basic section and construction technique set the standard for road construction in Europe until the late eighteenth century.[3]

After the collapse of the Roman Empire in 476 A.D., many Roman cities fell into a prolonged period of decline and decay. With the breakdown of administrative and political systems, controls over land eroded. Formerly public spaces such as streets were encroached upon. This erosion of the clear and regular Roman grid is seen in the evolution of the street patterns of Bologna, Verona, Naples, and many other cities built by the Romans. The superb paved Roman roadways deteriorated into an impassable ill-drained dirt road system, halting long distance vehicle travel. Carts and wagons were confined to farm and local use, while land travel was restricted to pedestrians or horses. Surviving cities struggled with repair and rebuilding of their defenses. Most cities were contained by enclosing walls and a few major streets led from the gateways to a focal center. Local internal streets were

The typical Roman road consisted of layers of flat stones, crushed stones, gravel, and coarse sand mixed with lime. The top surface was smooth paving stones and mortar. Two central traffic lanes were bordered by curbs 2 feet wide and 18 inches tall. The outside lanes were for one-way traffic. This construction method was standard in Europe until the late eighteenth century. *(Aitken)*

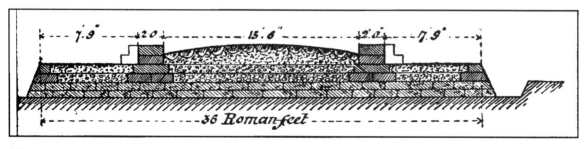

After the collapse of the Roman Empire, land controls weakened and the great Roman roads deteriorated. Encroachments into the public way were common. Streets became more irregular and often were little more than dark narrow passageways defined by tall building walls.
(© *Michael Southworth*)

merely narrow passageways defined by the building walls and overhead arches. Streets were flagged with stones and often incorporated steps to facilitate pedestrian movement.

The clear and regular Roman grid-iron found in cities like Bologna deteriorated in the Middle Ages, but fragments of the ancient grid pattern are still visible today. *(© Michael Southworth)*

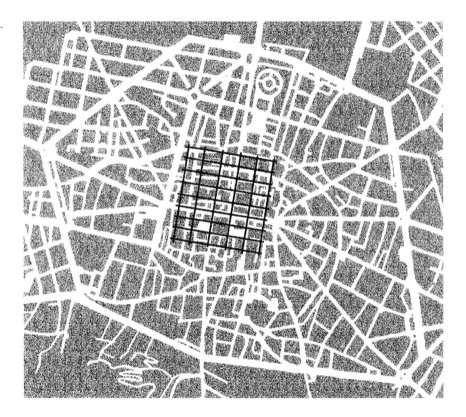

With the steady growth of towns and cities during the ninth and tenth centuries, overcrowding and congestion became a serious problem. Confined by existing defensive walls, buildings grew higher, and without public controls over construction and land use, individuals encroached on the street space. The lack of sanitary conveniences and regulations, along with deteriorating pavement, added to the hazardous and unhealthy conditions. Streets were filthy. As late as 1372, Parisians were permitted to throw waste from their windows whenever they chose after giving a warning by shouting three times.

By the eleventh century Europe entered an era of expanding population, travel, and trade. Although land routes remained largely neglected, sea navigation and exploration saw impressive advancement with the opening of trade to the Far East. As the power of the merchant class grew, they exerted pressure on the civic authorities to improve the street network.

With the revival of interest in the documents and monuments of antiquity during the thirteenth century, European architects such as Alberti, Palladio, Cataneo, and Scamozzi once again stressed the importance of well laid-out streets and approaches. Leon Battista Alberti (1404–1472), a major force in this revival, sought to advance the social and civic conditions of his time by studying ancient Classical architecture. For him, good architecture and city planning worked together, and encompassed skillful siting, regard for health conditions, adequate water supply, efficient construction techniques, thoughtful street layouts, and harmony of design. Alberti suggested two approaches to street planning according to the character of the city. In *De re aedificatoria*, his classic work on the laws of building, he wrote: "When they come to the Town, if the City is noble and powerful, the Streets should be strait and broad, which carries an Air of Greatness and Majesty; but if it is only a small Town or a Fortification, it will be better, and as safe, not for the Streets to run straight to the Gates; but to have them wind about sometimes to the Right, sometimes to the Left, near the Wall, and especially under the Towers upon the Wall; and within the Heart of Town, it will be handsomer not to have them strait, but winding about several Ways, backwards and forwards, like the Coarse of a River."[4]

Alberti stressed the practical application of winding streets as a means of protection and defense against an invading enemy. Yet he also acknowledged their aesthetic potential. "Moreover," he wrote, "this winding of the Streets will make the Passenger at every Step discover a new Structure, and the Front and the Door of every House will directly face the Middle of the Street; and whereas in larger Towns even too much Breadth is unhandsome and unhealthy, in a small one it will be both healthy and pleasant, to have such an open View from every House by Means of the Turn of the Street." He goes on to address the design of private streets: "The private ones should be like the publick; unless there be this Difference, that they be built exactly in strait Lines, which will answer better to the Corners of the Building, and the Divisions and Parts of the Houses. The Ancients in all Towns were for having some intricate Ways and turn-again Streets, without any Passage through

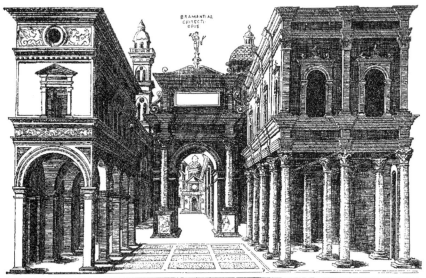

Renaissance architects envisioned orderly and balanced streets defined by Classical architecture. The simple geometry of the straight street was appealing for its pure form, as well as the opportunity to open up dramatic views to distant architectural elements. This view is attributed to Bramante. *(Muentz)*

Galeazzo Alessi designed Strada Nuova, an early example of the Renaissance straight street, in 1550 in Genoa, Italy. Grand palaces of the new merchant class were symmetrically arranged along the narrow paved street. *(in* American Vitruvius, *1922)*

them, that if an Enemy comes into them, he may be at a Loss, and be in Confusion and Suspence; or if he pushes on daringly, may be easily destroyed."[5]

The simple geometry of the straight street appealed to Renaissance architects for its pure form, as well as its potential for opening up dramatic perspectives to civic or religious landmarks. Military strategists also argued that the straight street would facilitate control in times of civil unrest or invasion. Thus, straight streets were inserted into the medieval urban maze. At the request of the Doge, architect Galeazzo Alessi (1512–1572) designed an early example of the straight street, Strada Nuova, in Genoa in 1550. This monumental street, which survives today as Via Garibaldi, was lined with the grand palaces of the new merchant class. The design specified uniform size and alignments of the palaces along the 25-foot-wide paved street, with entrances placed symmetrically opposite. New bourgeois suburbs designed in the form of rectilinear gridirons were attached to the old cities. Turin

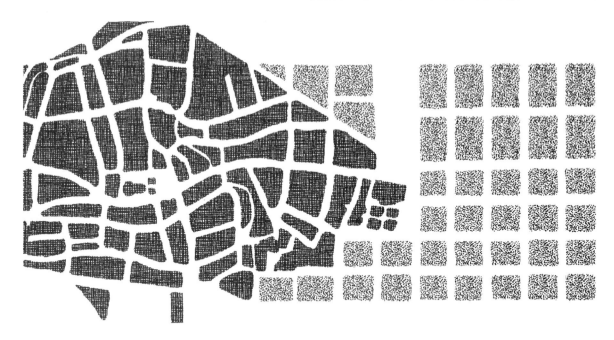

added three grid extensions to its Roman core, and later, Berlin and Vienna, along with many other cities, also added grid suburbs.

Andreas Palladio (1518–1580), another Italian architect inspired by Roman planning and architecture, envisioned an ideal city street. It was to be paved and would divide "the place where men are to walk, from that which serves for the use of carts and of cattle." In order to protect pedestrians from heat and rain, Palladio recommended the construction of porticos on both sides of the street: "I should like that the streets were divided, that on one and

As cities grew in the Renaissance, new bourgeois suburbs in gridiron patterns extended the medieval city. Ystad in southern Sweden added a Rennaissance extension to its organic core.
(© Michael Southworth)

Andreas Palladio (1508–1580), an Italian architect of the sixteenth century, recommended a paved street for pedestrians at least 8 feet wide and lined with trees outside the city gate. Lanes on each side surfaced in sand and gravel were for carriages and cattle. *(Palladio)*

17

Pierre-Marie-Jerome Tresaguet (1716–1796), the head of the first organization of civil engineers in Europe, developed a new road construction technique in 1775. Much lighter than the massive Roman design, it used subsoil and compacted broken fine stone on top of a base of square stones to support the load. *(Aitken)*

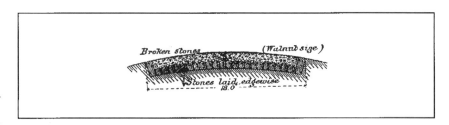

on the other part there were porticos made, through which the citizens might, under cover, go and do their business, without being molested by the sun, by the rains and snow."[6] To ensure drainage the street was concave in the middle and the sidewalks slanted toward the street.

Outside the city gates, Palladio recommended that streets have a minimum width of 8 feet (2.4 m) and be lined with trees on either side. Unlike the inner city streets, the center had a crowned, paved surface for the sole use of pedestrians. The two sides were made of sand and gravel for use by carriages and cattle. A stone curb separated the two areas and incorporated large milestones.

The French also contributed to the standardization of streets. In 1716, Louis XIV formed a body of road and bridge experts and engineers—the Corps des Ponts et Chaussées—to supervise public work. This was the first body of civil engineers in Europe maintained by a government. An associated school, the first professional civil engineering school in Europe, was established in 1738. In 1775, Pierre-Marie-Jerome Tresaguet, the head engineer for the board, developed a new type of relatively light road surface to replace the massive Roman cross section that was still in use. It was designed on the principle that the subsoil should support the load. Before this time roads were designed in the Roman manner to support heavy loads through thick pavements. Tresaguet's road section was constructed with compacted broken fine stone on top of a square stone base. The roadway crown rose 6 inches (15 cm) and had a consistent cross section of 18 feet (5.5 m).

In England, London's Westminister street improvement program created the first known "modern" city street section in 1765. Streets were lowered and leveled, and footpaths on each side were elevated, paved, and defined by curbstones. The carriageway was paved with smooth granite sloping to small drainage channels on both sides of the curbs.[7] In 1816, John Loudon McAdam, the general surveyor of Bristol, started a road building program utilizing his design for a new surface. His method used well-drained, compacted subgrade soil to support the load while the top layer acted only as a wearing surface to shed water. The 18-foot (5.5-m) crowned carriageway had only 10 inches (25 cm) of surfacing material, consisting of broken stones in small angular fragments not more than 2 inches (5 cm) in diameter laid in loose layers that were compacted under traffic. His solution was widely accepted, and by 1820 more than 125,000 miles (200,000 km) of roads were surfaced in England using this method. Modern-day macadam, derived from this approach, is now used worldwide.

John Loudon McAdam (1756–1836), the general surveyor of Bristol, England, invented a new system of road construction that now bears his name: macadam. A wearing surface of crushed rock was placed on top of well-drained, compacted subsoil. *(U.S. Department of Transportation, Federal Highway Administration)*

Early road and street building in North America was limited to colonial settlements and trading trails. By the seventeenth century road and street building paralleled that of England. Archeological excavations point to Pemaquid in Bristol Township, Maine, founded in 1625, as the first known site of a paved American city street. Built according to European prototypes, the street was paved with large stones. Archeologist John Henry Cartland describes it as "a short section of street about ten feet above high water mark, leading down a fine easy sloping field toward a small beach. . . . The larger stones form what we term the main street, which is thirty-three feet in width including the gutters, or water courses. . . . No prettier place could have been found along the shore, and it was in close proximity to the fort."[8]

The first engineered road in the United States was a private toll turnpike from Philadelphia to Lancaster, Pennsylvania, constructed in 1795. Its 62-mile (100-km) length was 20 feet (6 m)wide and was covered with broken stone and gravel. It lacked curbs but had cleared unpaved shoulders on both sides. A major act of road improvement in the United States was initiated in 1816 with the creation of the first American State Board of Public Works in Virginia, headed by Colonel Loammi Baldwin, the pioneering engineer known as the "father of civil engineering in America." The act provided for a corporate body with the power and funding to undertake public projects supervised by a principal engineer or surveyor. Soon after, a similar action was passed in South Carolina in 1817 and in Kentucky in 1835. The main result of these actions was improvements in resurfacing using the McAdam technique, which was first used in Maryland in 1823. With major railroad building worldwide, road building was virtually brought to a halt over the next 60 years, 1840–1900, and was confined to essential urban resurfacing improvements.

Colonel Loammi Baldwin (1780-1838), known as the "father of civil engineering in America," headed the American State Board of Public Works in Virginia, the first such organization in America, and initiated many road improvements. *(Illustrated History of Lowell and Vicinity, 1897)*

Street building in American colonial towns was limited, but by the seventeenth century they were paved in gravel or large stones, following English practice. *(© Michael Southworth)*

The first macadam road in America was built in 1823 between Hagerstown and Boonsboro, Maryland. The finished surface was 15 inches thick at the center and 20 feet wide. It completed the last unimproved gap in the road leading from Baltimore on the Chesapeake Bay to Wheeling on the Ohio River. (*U.S. Department of Transportation, Federal Highway Administration*)

THE FIRST SUBURBS
IN ENGLAND

During the industrial period in Britain, urban road design and improvement often were responses to crowding and degradation of the urban environment. The *Report on Conditions of the Laboring Classes in the Town of Leeds* (1845) states: "Let the poor family, consisting of a man, his wife, and five children, two or three of whom are adolescent, be imagined occupying one of these chambers, in a cul-de-sac, or in an undrained and unpaved street, seven human beings, each requiring 600 cubic feet of breathing room, shut up in a chamber not containing more than 1000 feet for the whole. . . both parents and children rising in winter and summer at five o'clock in the morning and laboring in other unhealthy atmospheres. . . and returning to the limited atmosphere of the night, unchanged, because unable to be improved, owing to the defective sanitary regulation, or an entire absence of them; — and the mind that so thinks, draws a picture which the theater of any large manufacturing town pourtray (sic) in thousands instances."[9] The exploitation of street space arose in the absence of any regulations or restraints to manage the environmental impacts from the growing population. In 1842 only 86 of the nearly 600 streets of Leeds were under municipal control and were sewered and paved.[10] In 1844, *the First Report of the Commissioners of the State of Large Towns and Population Districts*, published in London, advocated a fundamental rethinking of street design. Regulating street width and direction was seen as a key to controlling growth and ensuring long-term planning. The commission set up a hundred year program: "The widening and straightening of streets should be done in concert, rather than leaving improvement to an occasional widening project. The determining feature in each street would be an imaginary center line drawn on an official map from which all building lines could be controlled in the future. As the old houses became ruinous they would be pulled down and new structures erected farther back."[11]

To avoid the harsh physical and social conditions of the industrial city, affluent citizens chose to live in new developments at the rural–urban edge. The origins of this urban edge suburbia may be traced to late eighteenth and early nineteenth century London. Wealthy bankers and merchants were starting to experiment with a variety of different housing forms that reflected their changing attitudes toward the industrial city. The intensity of life in the mixed-class neighborhoods and the physical conditions of the urban environment fueled the search for segregation. The bourgeoisie wanted neighborhoods that were both class segregated and purely residential, focusing on the emerging nuclear family.[12] These families wanted to separate themselves from the intrusion of the workplace and the city on their lives and thus sought a separation between places of work and residence. The London elite began to abandon their combined home and offices in the heart of the city, moving their families out of town to large villas in the agricultural fringe that ringed the city. They realized that "with their private carriages and ample funds, they were no longer limited to the area traditionally considered the city. On relatively inexpensive land still a surprisingly short commute to the core, they could build a world of privilege, leisure, and family life that reflected their values."[13]

As the suburban notion trickled down from the elite to the middle class, the demand for more building sites increased. Coincidentally, landowners at the edge of the city profited from the new living pattern. Their challenge was to design communities that would satisfy the new buyers' aspirations. John Nash had the answer.

JOHN NASH
AND PARK VILLAGE

The origins of the idyllic suburb are found in painting, philosophy, and literature of the seventeenth and eighteenth century which idealized rural values and picturesque landscapes. Toward the end of the eighteenth century landscape gardeners, builders, and architects began experimenting with the ideas in their work. Between 1790 and 1810 over one hundred patternbooks for picturesque cottages appeared. Among the leaders of the picturesque movement in design in Britain were architect John Nash and landscape gardener Humphrey Repton. Born in 1752 in humble circumstances, Nash was the son of a Welsh millwright, but he worked his way up into British society, eventually befriending many influential people including the Prince Regent himself. Nash was ambitious and courageous, as well as imaginative and witty, but he could also be pushy and somewhat lacking in refinement. In a letter to John Soane he described himself as having a "thick, squat, dwarf figure, with round head, snub nose, and little eyes."[14]

Credit for the first realization of the suburban ideal in physical form must be given to Nash, who was much taken with applying the picturesque to architectural and urban design problems. His earliest project for exploring

John Nash (1752–1835), an ambitious architect and friend of King George IV, promoted the picturesque approach to design. Among his many projects was the first suburb, Park Village, the forerunner of all later romantic suburbs. *(Royal Institute of British Architects)*

the picturesque in village form was Blaise Hamlet, an estate village in Gloucestershire near Bristol that he designed for J. S. Harford, a Quaker banker. Begun by 1810, it was to provide housing for Harford's retired servants. Harford was apparently enthusiastic about the picturesque landscape style, for in 1796 Humphrey Repton created for the estate one of his red-leather-bound "before–after" books, *The Red Book for Blaise*, which illustrated how the appearance of the estate might be improved. The Repton thread continued in Nash's work when Repton's son George Stanley Repton assisted Nash in his work on Blaise Hamlet. Nash placed the village in a wooded area on the estate and set the nine rustic cottages on irregularly shaped lots arranged informally along a narrow road winding around the central green. Carefully designed siting allowed views to unfold as one moved through the tiny village, with much hidden from any one vantage point. Each cottage had unique design features: elaborate chimneys, thatched or slate roofs, hips, gables, overhangs, dormers, bay windows, and much use of climbing ivy, woodbine, roses, and jasmine.

The qualities of the romantic village are well expressed in the travel journal of Hermann Pückler-Muskau, a German prince who admired Nash and his work. Except for the poverty-stricken residents, the images he described might be of a suburb of much later vintage. On his visit to Blaise Hamlet in 1828 he wrote of a beautiful green in the wood: ". . . on it are built nine cottages, all of different forms and materials . . . each surrounded with different trees, and enwreathed with various sorts of clematis, rose, honeysuckle, and vine. The dwellings, which are perfectly detached though they form a whole, have separate gardens, and a common fountain, which stands in the centre of the green, overshadowed by old trees. . . . The gardens, divided by neat hedges, form a pretty garland of flowers and herbs around the whole village. What crowns the whole is, that the inhabitants are all poor families, whom the generous proprietor allows to live in the houses rent-free. No more delightful or well-chosen spot could be found as a refuge for misfortune: its perfect seclusion and snugness breathe only peace and forgetfulness of the world."[15] Blaise Hamlet, meant to be a serene place of retirement, became an attraction almost immediately. Today it is a National Trust Property.

As a friend of the Prince Regent (who became George IV in 1820) Nash received choice commissions and was appointed architect to the Office of Woods and Forests. Nash's ideas for a new park and street—Regent's Park and Regent's Street—on the former Marylebone Park, a Crown property, so impressed the Prince Regent with their originality that in 1810 Nash was asked to prepare a plan. A picturesque conception, the park was to have 56 scattered villas in a garden setting, featuring changing views of landscape and architectural elements, with monumental scenic rows of houses and apartments defining the edges.

Intrigued by the picturesque village he had created for Blaise and for his own amusement, Nash decided to try the idea in a more urban setting at the northeast edge of the new park on the rapidly developing fringe of London.

The picturesque movement promoted rural values and images. Over 100 patternbooks for picturesque cottages were published between 1790 and 1810. These drawings are from W.S. Pocock's 1807 handbook *Architectural Designs for Rustic Cottages, Picturesque Dwellings, Villas, &c. (Pocock, The Environmental Design Library, University of California at Berkeley)*

Whole villages such as Nash's
Blaise Hamlet were built in the pic-
turesque style. This view is an
imagined cottage in a village from
P.F. Robinson's 1823 handbook
*Rural Architecture or a Series of
Designs for Ornamental Cottages.*
*(Robinson, The Environmental
Design Library, University of
California at Berkeley)*

The result was Park Village, a more urban picturesque village than Blaise
Hamlet and the forerunner of later romantic suburbs. The nearby district of
St. John's Wood, a London suburb with a plan dating from 1794 but devel-
oped at about the same time as Park Village, was the first district of London
to adopt the detached and semi-detached house in place of the row house.
Park Village actually consisted of two parts, since it straddled the Regent's
Canal which was built as an extension of the Grand Junction Canal to bring
goods via barge and boat to the markets and docks. The canal also served as
a picturesque element in Regent's Park and as a source of water for the lake.
One of Nash's last projects, the plan for Park Village East, dates from 1823
and construction began the next year when Nash was 72. His plan avoided
the formal eighteenth-century urban pattern of solid streets and squares.
Instead the houses were set within a picturesque landscape. All of the elements of the picturesque suburb are contained in the scheme: a winding street
with sidewalks, houses of varied styles, unfolding views, and landscape features such as water elements, trees, and changes of terrain. Most houses were
built in pairs to look like mansions. Half of the original 50 houses were
demolished when the railway was widened in 1900–1906 and the Park
Village segment of Regent's Canal is now filled in.

Park Village West, off Albany Street, has fared much better and is an
exquisite jewel of neighborhood design still delightful today. Arranged along
a narrow loop street, each house is different, including detached and semi-
detached houses, as well as a row of very small houses. Views unfold as one
moves through it, with Tower House serving as a pivotal focus from both

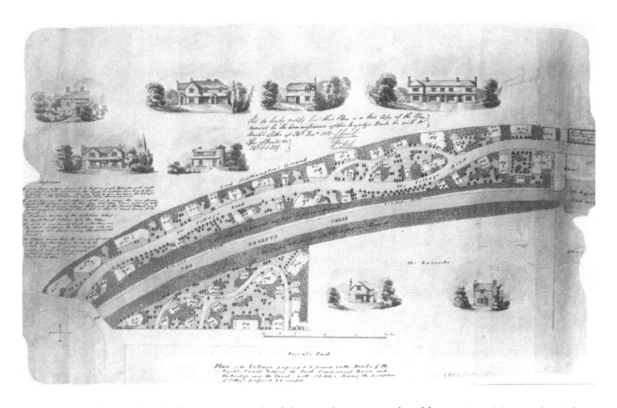

directions. After Nash's death in 1835 much of this work was completed by Nash's protegé and successor, James Pennethorne.

After his patron George IV died in 1830, Nash's numerous detractors, including the Duke of Wellington, did everything they could to "make a hash of Nash" and he was abruptly dismissed from his commission to convert Buckingham House into a palace. He retired to his country house and died in 1835. The Victorians hated him and what he stood for, and only in this century have his achievements been recognized. Nash's design for Park Village responded to those seeking to live at what was then the rural edge of the city. He was able to synthesize and borrow from a range of styles and translate them into a picturesque village within a parklike yet urban setting. Nash's ability to integrate scattered elements of the suburban style into a working formula transformed the suburban development into a reproducible product.

John Nash began work on Park Village East in 1823. Situated at the growth edge of London, it offered detached and semidetached homes in a parklike setting along the Regents Canal adjacent to Regents Park. All of the elements of the picturesque suburb are present. *(Public Record Office, London)*

OLMSTED, VAUX, AND THE AMERICAN SUBURB

Expansion of the railroad system in the United States, beginning in the mid-nineteenth century, was a major force in urbanization and brought with it the ubiquitous rectilinear gridiron plan. Standardized town plats were often used repeatedly—in Illinois, the same plat map was used thirty-three times! As industrialization spread across America antiurban attitudes took root. Several influential authors helped shape American attitudes toward subur-

The curving streets of Park Village were an important ingredient of the picturesque suburb. *(Guildhall Library, London)*

Park Village East street section, 1823. *(© Eran Ben-Joseph)*

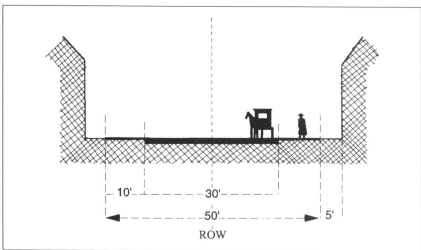

ban living including Catherine Beecher, Andrew Downing, Calvert Vaux, and Frederick Law Olmsted. Catherine Esther Beecher (the sister of Harriet Beecher Stowe) was the eldest child of Lyman Beecher, a clergyman and a liberal theologian who fought against slavery and intemperance. An early advocate of education for women, she believed in the moral superiority of women and the separation between female and a male spheres of life. Among her twenty-five published books, none was more influential than the popular *Treatise on Domestic Economy, For the Use of Young Ladies at Home and at School*, published in 1841. Through her writings Beecher promoted an ideal family life set in a one- or two-story cottage nestled in a semirural environment.

Streets of Park Village West are narrow and winding so that views unfold. Most homes were built in pairs to look like mansions.
(© *Michael Southworth*)

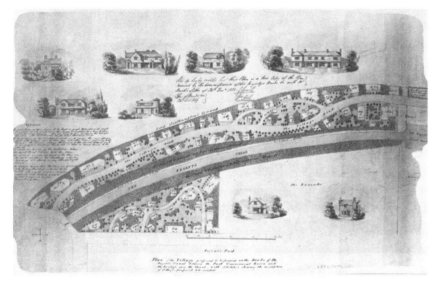

Detail Plan of Park Village West
(*Public Record Office, London*)

Similar to Beecher, landscape designer Andrew Jackson Downing, saw the benefit in advocating suburban country living in America as a way to establish moral influence, cultural order, and the reconstruction of social structure. In 1850 he wrote: "When smiling lawns and tasteful cottages begin

The development of the railroad brought with it a standardized approach to street layout. The grid-iron pattern was used almost exclusively, being easy to survey and lay out, and simple to subdivide. *(© William Garnett)*

With the vast amounts of land given to the railroads by the federal government in return for developing the system, railroad companies were actually in the business of land development. Using standardized town plat maps, they could lay out a town and auction lots in a matter of days. The Illinois Central used the same plat map to make 33 different towns. *(Baker Library, Historical Collections, Harvard Business School)*

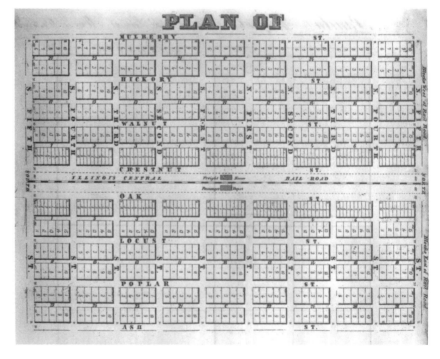

In reaction to industrialization in the nineteenth century, many designers and writers sought a return to a more rural existence. Catherine Beecher, sister of Harriet Beecher Stowe, wrote influential books on housekeeping in the mid-nineteenth century that promoted suburban living. *The American Woman's Home* portrays the ideal "Healthful and Economical House" as a picturesque dwelling in a rural landscape. *(The Bancroft Library, University of California at Berkeley)*

Frederick Law Olmsted
(1822–1903), designer of New
York's Central Park and Boston's
Emerald Necklace, was an ardent
advocate of suburban living.
*(Courtesy of the National Park
Service, Frederick Law Olmsted
National Historic Site)*

Calvert Vaux (1824–1895) came
from England to work with
Olmsted on numerous projects such
as New York Central Park and
Riverside, Illinois. *(Courtesy of the
National Park Service, Frederick
Law Olmsted National Historic
Site)*

to embellish a country, we know that order and culture are established . . . the individual home has a great social value for people. Whatever new system may be needed for the regeneration of the old and enfeebled nation, we are persuaded that, in America, not only is the distinct family the best social form, but those elementary forces which give rise to the genius and the finest character may, for the most part, be traced back to the farm house and the rural cottage. . . . It is the solitude and freedom of the family home in the country which constantly preserves the purity of . . . the nation, and invigorates its intellectual powers."[16]

The English picturesque tradition of design strongly influenced American architects and designers such as Andrew Downing, Calvert Vaux, and Frederick Law Olmsted. Both Downing and Olmsted visited Europe around 1850, and Downing convinced Vaux, who was born in England, to come and practice in the United States. Olmsted was interested in the new English design trends as manifested in the work of Joseph Paxton (1803–1865) and John Nash. During a visit to London and Liverpool in 1850 he encountered the prototypes for his later work as a park designer and suburban planner— Birkenhead Park and its surrounding suburb. With its curving roads and picturesque layouts it typified the traditions of English suburban design and provided Olmsted with the principles he was to apply in the United States.

Olmsted's experience as an urban designer while working on New York City's Central Park further strengthened his belief in suburban living. Reflecting upon urban dwelling conditions, he stated that in suburbia "there are to be found among them the most attractive, the most refined and the most soundly wholesome forms of domestic life, and the best application of the arts of civilization to which mankind has yet attained. It would appear then, that the demands of suburban life, with reference to civilized refinement, are not to be a retrogression from, but an advance upon, those which are characteristic of town life, and that no great town can long exist without great suburbs."[17] Olmsted associated poor urban living conditions with the physical layouts of American cities. Along with landscape architect H. W. S. Cleveland, he criticized the gridiron street system for rectangular blocks with overcrowded row houses. Olmsted was even critical of the popular New York brownstone row houses which he described as: "a confession that it is impossible to build a convenient and tasteful residence in New York adapted to the civilized requirements of a single family, except at a cost which even rich men find prohibitive."[18] His rejection of the grid and the adoption of the curvilinear road and single family house epitomized the suburban ideal of the placid and pastoral in contrast to the efficient and mechanistic order of the urban environment.

One of Olmsted's earliest attempts in designing a suburban community came in 1866 with his proposal for a "Projected Improvment of the Estate of the College of California, at Berkeley, Near Oakland." Olmsted's layout was designed in juxtaposition to the existing rectangular blocks and streets around the college. He argued for a pristine and rustic neighborhood that

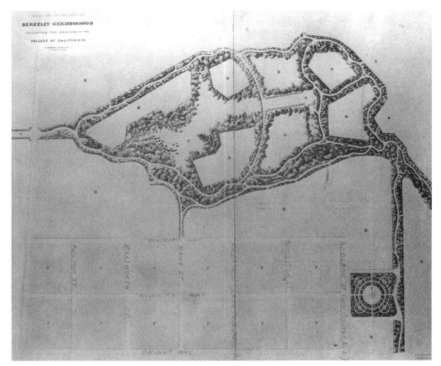

In 1866 Olmsted designed a Berkeley neighborhood that included the campus, one of his first attempts to design a suburban community. He paid particular attention to the natural topography and views when laying out the streets and lots. Piedmont Avenue (along the right edge of the plan) was the only part of the scheme built. *(The Bancroft Library, University of California at Berkeley)*

would provide "a suitable degree of seclusion and a suitable degree of association with the active life of that part of the world not given to the pursuit of scholars."[19] To attain the design objectives, Olmsted required a specific street layout for the neighborhood, with the streets following the natural topography while providing comfortable access and the best views from the homes. He wrote: "The main requirements of a plan, then, for the improvement of this region, with reference to residences, must be, first, so to arrange the roads upon which private property will front as to secure the best practicable landscape effect from the largest number of points of view; second, so to arrange the roads and public ground as to give the owners of the private property satisfactory outgoing, in respect, first, to convenience of use; second, to attractiveness in their borders; and, third, to command of occasional distant views and complete landscapes."[20]

Except for Piedmont Avenue, one of the major streets, the Berkeley project never materialized for financial reasons. Olmsted and Vaux finally realized their residential philosophy in their 1868 plan for the suburb of Riverside, Illinois, which turned a featureless 1,600-acre tract of "low, flat, miry, and forlorn land" into a picturesque landscaped community.[21] Tree-lined roads, "gracefully-curved lines, generous spaces, and the absence of sharp corners" were laid in deliberate contrast to the prevailing city street grid "to suggest and imply leisure, contemplativeness and happy tranquillity."[22] Houses were set back at least 30 feet (9.2 m) from the road to please the

Olmsted and Vaux finally realized their suburban vision in Riverside, Illinois in 1868. Their design transformed a featureless tract of land into a romantic, picturesque landscape. *(Courtesy of the National Park Service, Frederick Law Olmsted National Historic Site)*

eye. "We cannot judiciously attempt to control the form of the houses which men shall build, we can only, at most, take care that if they build very ugly and inappropriate houses, they shall not be allowed to force them disagreeably upon our attention when we desire to pass along the road upon which they stand. We can require that no house shall be built within a certain number of feet of the highway, and we can insist that each house-holder shall

Riverside street section. *(© Eran Ben-Joseph)*

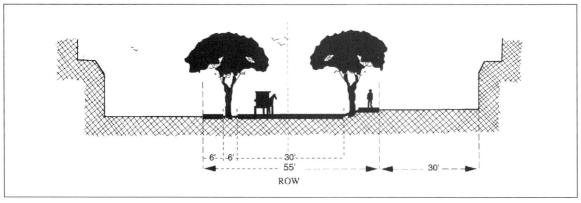

The 1871 promotional brochure for Riverside emphasized the quality of the street environment for carriage rides, as well as walking. *(Riverside Historical Museum)*

DRIVES.

Riverside completed will enjoy about 40 miles of carriage road, similar and equal to the drives in Central Park, N. Y., all made of easy grade, smooth surface, thoroughly drained, storm and frost proof, and equally serviceable and enjoyable in winter, spring and summer. A vast deal of expense and care is taken in the construction of these roads, by first taking off the vegetable matter of the soil to the clay or sand, then spreading broken stone to the depth of one foot over the entire surface of the roadway, this being covered with gravel to the depth of three inches, and then rolled to a firm and smooth surface. The Riverside Company imported from Europe a patent Steam Road Roller, weighing fifteen tons, which they have used in the construction of the completed roads at Riverside. Rollers of this description have been recently introduced into the Parks of London and Paris.

View of Long Common and Junction of Roads.

WALKS.

About eighty miles of walks will be required at Riverside, which are to be laid on either side of the roadways, along the river banks, and through the parks and borders. These walks are all properly graded, and are constructed of Trinidad asphalt, coal tar and gravel, laid and rolled when hot, making durable, firm, smooth and pleasant promenades.

The street design for Riverside became the prototype for American suburbs. Streets curve in a leisurely manner and are lined by trees planted in strips between the sidewalk and roadway. Houses are set back from the street at least 30 feet, so that the street landscape dominates the visual scene. *(Riverside Historical Commission)*

maintain one or two living trees between his house and his highway line."[23] The residential roadway was set at a width of 30 feet (9.2 m), with pedestrian walkways on both sides. Trees were planted in a strip between the path and the roadway, the first time Olmsted and Vaux systematically carried out this feature in the suburban context. This form of road planting as a physical and visual separator between road and pedestrian was probably influenced by the planting design schemes of Haussmann's Paris boulevards of the 1860s and became a prominent feature in the American suburban landscape. In the next decades Olmsted and his followers designed and built suburbs of similar design across the country including Brookline, Massachusetts, Forest Hills Gardens in Queens, the Country Club District of Kansas City, and Palos Verdes in Los Angeles.

Orderly Streets for Healthy Cities

Social Response to Urban Disorder

While standardization of the width and arrangement of streets is a convenient, labor-saving method of regulating the subdivision of real estate, it cannot be held to show much foresight.

—Charles Mulford Robinson, 1911

During the late nineteenth century the environmental chaos of the city was considered to be linked to its social problems. Overcrowding and deteriorating sanitary conditions were believed to cause social and moral degeneration. Social and health reformers argued that the inevitable social disorder would be controlled best by improving the environment: "Experience has shown that people living in clean, quiet, orderly streets, in tenements well kept, both as to sanitary arrangements and cleanliness, keep, as a general thing, their own apartments neat and clean, and also that their whole bearing is one of self-respect."[1] As reformers discovered the difficulty of improving the inner city, many began advocating dispersed multi-centered growth patterns.

Fore Street, Lambeth (London) in the 1860s. The filthy, congested streets of industrial cities prompted reform movements and new street standards. *(Victoria and Albert Museum)*

Dispersal of the population from the city center would be the perfect solution to the urban dilemma. Suburbanization was seen as a vital force not only in urbanizing the countryside, but also in revitalizing the city. Some saw the suburbs as representing a shift of emphasis from property to people: "A one or two room tenement, sunless, almost airless, and at a cost that would pay for a comfortable home in an attractive suburb, is worse than a travesty. It is almost a crime."[2] Suburbia might also offer a better life for the industrial worker: "The suburbanizing of the wage earner is a great social and economic opportunity. . . . It is for us to say whether this growth will result in a contamination of open country by the city slums or whether garden communities will look upon the bleak horrors of our urbanized existence and give men, women, and children a new lease on life and industry and a chance to

Bandits Roost, Mulberry Bend, New York, 1888. Jacob Riis documented the squalid conditions of New York streets. *(Riis Collection, Museum of the City of New York)*

serve men rather than enslave them . . . . The Utopian city of yesterday can be realized in the growing suburbs of our own times."[3]

The demand for better living conditions—light, air, cleanliness, and relief from street congestion—prompted intervention by public authority. In England, the Public Health Act of 1875 established the "Bye-law" [sic] Street Ordinance. The vision of wide, straight, paved streets entranced the authorities who saw it as the best solution for the ills of their cities. Inspired by European neoclassic urban design of the seventeenth century with its uniformity and order, they mistakenly adopted it to remedy industrial city conditions. In one project in Leeds, 238 inhabitants were removed and 59 dwellings were dismantled to provide more street space.[4] Unfortunately, the uniformity of the layout and the rigidity of the design were inappropriate for a residential environment: "Nothing remained of the past intimacy . . . nor are there any mitigating effects from nature—no intervening grass or trees between the street and the houses. The street space is swept so clean as to approach emotional emptiness and complete negation."[5]

Although the English by-law street design did not answer residential social needs, its basic principles stressing the importance of light, air, and access nevertheless remained prominent. By-law developments spread throughout the industrial cities of Britain including London and survive today in districts like Fulham, which experienced gentrification in the 1980s. They may be found in their purest, most dreary expression in West Ham and East Ham. Typically, by-law streets are very long, straight, and are arranged within a grid of parallel streets. Rather monotonous in overall feeling, they are framed by brick rowhouses, two to three stories tall, identical in layout and style. However, treatments vary from block to block. In Fulham, one street may have one-story bay windows, while on another they may be two stories; one street may have trees, and another may have none. The main element that

THE "BYE-LAW" STREET

As their model for new street standards, nineteenth century British reformers looked to neoclassic urban design of Europe. The straight, uniform streets of Friedrich Weinbrenner's 1808 design were clean and orderly, but offered little public amenity. *(Friedrich Weinbrenner)*

37

Before the Bye-law Street
Ordinance of 1875, greater London
had many semirural districts like
Fulham with its market gardens,
farms, and small village centers.
*(Wyld's New Plan of London,
1867, The Bancroft Library,
University of California at
Berkeley)*

The enormous pressures for housing and the Bye-law Ordinance
transformed districts like Fulham
into monotonous gridded neighborhoods with little public amenity.
(Raymond Unwin)

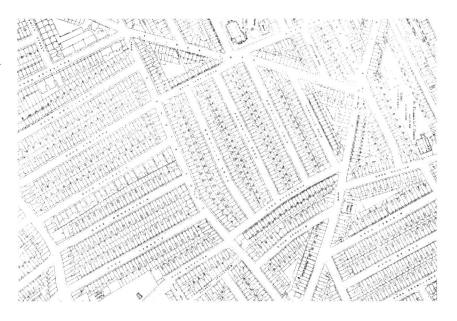

The typical by-law street was long, straight, and lined by rowhouses of uniform design. Street trees were rare. (© *Michael Southworth*)

lends variety within a street is the color the brick facades are painted. The major impact of the Bye-law Street Ordinance was establishment of the right-of-way of 40 to 50 feet (12.2–15.25 m) as a standard configuration for residential street widths, a standard still used today.

At the time the Bye-law [sic] Street Ordinance came into effect in 1875, developer Jonathan T. Carr acquired 24 acres of orchard land west of London with the intention of building a suburban community, Bedford Park. Carr and his architect, E. W. Godwin, recognized the potential of the large existing trees and rejected the idea of bare and clean by-law streets laid out in a uniform pattern. Their scheme responded to the natural pattern of the plantation. Organized around a small green with a church and a few shops near Turnham Green Station, Bedford Park was promoted as "The Healthiest Place in the World."[6] Sometimes called "the first garden suburb," it is a comfortable, intimately scaled district with good access to local shops, services, and transportation. Streets roughly radiate from the village green and have sidewalks and planting strips on both sides. Although the development is small, the streets offer many different visual experiences because of the varied architecture and irregular street pattern. Streets usually bend or terminate with a view of buildings rather than open street, creating a very intimate, village feeling. Although the street right-of-way remained at 40 feet (12.2 m), the actual paved area of most streets is only 26 feet (8 m) and there is parking on both sides. Houses are set back 12 to 20 feet (4–6 m), allowing small front yards or courts that create an effective transition between house and street, private and public. Many of the houses were designed by Norman Shaw in Queen Anne Revival style in red brick with white trim of wood.

BEDFORD PARK ADAPTS THE BYE-LAW STREET

Norman Shaw designed many of the houses in Bedford Park in Queen Anne Revival style.

E. W. Godwin tried to avoid the barren monotony of the by-law developments in his plan for Bedford Park in 1875. Sometimes called the first garden suburb, the streets radiate from the village green and transit station. Most streets bend or terminate with a view of buildings rather than open street. *(Hounslow Library Network, Local Studies Collection, Chiswick Library)*

Bedford Park streets are narrow and lined by trees and sidewalks. *(© Eran Ben-Joseph)*

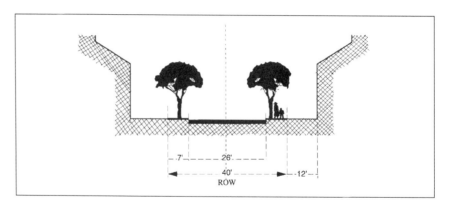

The architecture of Bedford Park avoided the monotony of the by-law developments. The Queen Anne Revival houses of red brick with white trim have much variety in design and detail, although only nine building types were used. *(Hounslow Library Network, Local Studies Collection, Chiswick Library)*

Although there are only nine building types, there is plentiful exterior architectural variety in the design of porches, fences, gates, dormers, gables, bay windows, and chimneys. Primarily row houses and semidetached pairs, they are are often designed to look like large single-family houses. Since there were no garages in the late nineteenth century, cars usually park on the street or in a paved front court converted from the original entry garden.

The mature preserved trees were a powerful unifying element that set Bedford Park apart from the more conventional suburbs around London.

The Bedford Park street design, as well as its architectural design, created a livable yet compact neighborhood that is still one of London's more desirable places to live. (© Michael Southworth)

According to *Chamber's Journal* of 1881: "The peculiar characteristic of these streets is the utter absence of that stiffness which always seems to attend the chilly regular, and hideous house-rows of our other suburbs."[7] "All the others [roads] appear closed at the end by trees and houses, and form a succession of views, as if the architect has taken a hint from Nature."[8] The Bedford Park street layout provided the first challenge to the by-law street. With its rejection of straight vistas, barren width, and uniformity, Bedford Park inspired succeeding suburban street designers to question authoritative prescriptions. It has stood the test of time and today it is still one of London's more delightful and livable neighborhoods.

UNWIN, PARKER, AND THE GARDEN CITIES

Henrietta Barnett, a vicar's wife who had lived in London's impoverished East End, conceived the idea of a new, healthful community with good housing for the less well-off on the edge of London. Her dream was realized when Raymond Unwin and Barry Parker were commissioned to design the suburban community of Hampstead Garden Suburb near Hampstead in Golder's Green in 1904. Unwin and Parker consciously revived motifs that had been outlawed by earlier by-law regulations. Their design challenged the impersonal monotonous layouts of the by-law streets, and returned to the intimate and refined spatial forms of courts and yards associated with traditional communities. Unwin argued: "Another bye-law [sic] which is not uncommon is that against roads having no through way, known as cul-de-sac roads. This action has, no doubt, been taken to avoid unwholesome yards; but for residential purposes, particularly since the development of the motor-car, the cul-de-sac roads, far from being undesirable, are especially to be desired for those who like quiet for their dwellings."[9] Unwin felt that the physical form of street and building layouts directly influenced social behavior and the well-being of the community. A persistent man, he lobbied for the "Hampstead Garden Suburban Act," a private bill passed by Parliament in 1906 that suspended certain building regulations. The bill allowed creation of cul-de-sacs and permitted roads of less than 500 feet (152 m) in length with carriageway widths enormously reduced from 35 feet (10.6 m) to 12 and 16 feet (3.6–4.9 m).

Unwin and Parker's attempts to change land development regulations and approaches grew out of their desire to translate their social and aesthetic beliefs into physical form. According to Unwin, they found their architectural inspiration in the German town planning principles of Dr. Josef Stübben, the American civic art of Charles Mulford Robinson, and especially the writings of Viennese architect Camillo Sitte, author of *Der Stadtebau* (1889). Sitte initiated the theory that the informal urban patterns of the Middle Ages possessed compositional qualities that were more in tune with human aspirations than formal geometrical configurations. Thinking of such possibilities, Unwin wrote: "There can be no doubt that much of the interest of the old irregular streets and towns lies in the sense of their free, spontaneous growth, their gradual extension under changing influences, much of which must be lacking in the case of a town built to order and according to a prearranged plan."[10]

Ebenezer Howard's *To-morrow: A Peaceful Path to Real Reform* published in 1898 (later published as *Garden Cities of To-morrow* in 1902) provided the theoretical framework of social integration with the physical well-being of society. As a social reformer, Howard advocated a new economic and social order, a new society: "Town and country must be married,

Raymond Unwin (1863–1940), along with Barry Parker, challenged the by-law regulations in the design for Hampstead Garden Suburb in 1904. *(Royal Institute of British Architects)*

Unwin and Parker were inspired by the town planning ideas of Viennese architect Camillo Sitte. Sitte admired the informal, unpredictable spatial qualities of European towns of the Middle Ages, which seemed to develop spontaneously, without an overall plan, such as this street in old Rouen. *(© Michael Southworth)*

and out of this joyous union will spring a new hope, a new life, a new civilization."[11] His utopian dream was to be manifested in "a town designed for healthy living and industry; of a size that makes possible a full measure of social life, but not larger; surrounded by a rural belt; the whole of the land being in public ownership or held in trust for the community."[12]

Unwin and Parker attempted to realize Howard's goals of social reform in their design for Hampstead Garden Suburb, emphasizing the integration of different classes by providing many different unit types and sizes: "The growing up of suburbs occupied solely by any individual class is bad, socially, economically, and aesthetically . . . . If, then, the site that is being planned is one which we expect mainly to have a working class population, we should still try to arrange some attractive corner in which a few rather large houses

The layout of Hampstead Garden Suburb avoided the rectilinear grid and utilized numerous cul-de-sacs and courts to create quiet pedestrian-oriented residential enclaves. *(Raymond Unwin)*

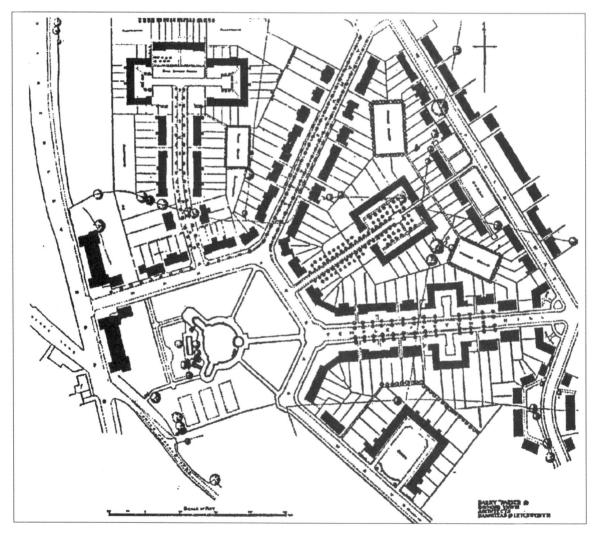

may be built; we should induce the doctor to live among his patients by affording him a suitable site, and give an opportunity for those who have been successful in life, to live in suitable homes among others not so fortunate. And whether or not we shall succeed will depend very much upon the arrangement."[13] Not as cozy and comfortable as Bedford Park, and much larger, Hampstead Garden Suburb consists mainly of two-family semidetached houses, row houses, and apartments, with few single-family houses. The architects' fascination with the German medieval town is evident in the steeply pitched roofs, decorative gables, and wrought iron details.

The annulment of the Bye-law Street Ordinance in Hampstead allowed Unwin to experiment with a variety of street forms and configurations that he believed would support the concept of a community such as those envisioned by the Garden City movement. The street pattern studiously avoids the rectilinear grid, and similar to Bedford Park, has radial streets eminating from the village green near the tube station on Finchley Road, a commercial corridor: "The roadways in Hampstead ignore right angles. They avoid regularity in every way. They meander about aimlessly, comfortably, following the natural contour and advantages of the land. Nor are they of equal width. The residential streets are narrow. They are designed to discourage traffic and keep it on the main thoroughfares."[14]

For the first time a planned development systematically used the cul-de-sac and open court throughout. In the court and close arrangements, two- to three-story blocks of rowhouses or apartments define a central green space and are usually accessed by a narrow service road. This arrangement creates a relatively quiet, pedestrian-oriented environment that is removed from the public street, a semiprivate milieu of some architectural distinction. The cul-de-sacs achieve similar residential neighborhood values. Unlike the American

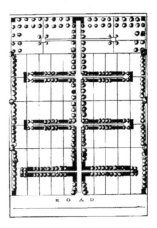

Unwin and Parker were strong advocates of the residential cul-de-sac, but an Act of Parliament was required to build them in Hampstead Garden Suburb. *(Raymond Unwin)*

Street section, Hampstead Garden Suburb. *(© Eran Ben-Joseph)*

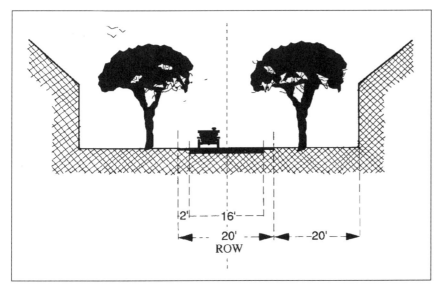

Streets in Hampstead Garden Suburb are generally very narrow, with a 13- to 16-foot pavement within a 20-foot right-of-way. *(Raymond Unwin)*

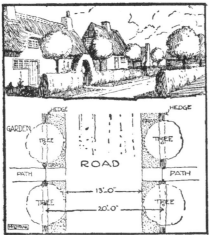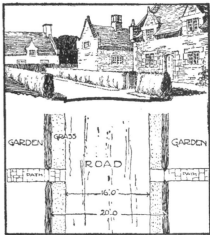

In this early view of Hampstead Garden Suburb, the narrow street is surfaced in gravel and has no curbs. The road serves both pedestrians and vehicles. *(Raymond Unwin)*

Today most streets have sidewalks and two lanes of traffic, as well as parking and street trees, all neatly fit into the narrow right-of-way. *(© Michael Southworth)*

The residential courts of Hampstead Garden Suburb offer a quiet, semiprivate setting. (© *Michael Southworth*)

Unlike cul-de-sacs of American suburbs, the Hampstead Garden Suburb cul-de-sacs are narrow and have no circular turn-around at the end. Pedestrian ways continue through the cul-de-sacs to paths beyond, making a well-connected and interesting pedestrian network. (© *Michael Southworth*)

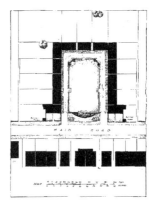

Some of the housing is arranged in courts of two- to three-story rowhouses or apartments surrounding a common green space, lined by a narrow service road. (*Raymond Unwin*)

postwar cul-de-sac, these are short and narrow, with no circular turn-around at the end. Typically, midblock pedestrian walks connect from the end of the cul-de-sac to another street or cul-de-sac beyond, making a well-connected and interesting path network for the pedestrian. Road types are hierarchical and are designed to discourage through traffic; they vary in both layout and cross-section according to function. Sidewalks are always present and are made interesting by the adjacent planting of trees and shrubs, as well as architectural details such as walls, fences, and gates that make each street a unique and interesting pedestrian path. Hampstead Garden Suburb thus became a major prototype for residential subdivision street design and road planning.

47

CHARLES MULFORD
ROBINSON
AND THE STREET AS A
WORK OF ART

Unlike European scholars and designers who saw the remedy for urban problems in the creation of garden suburbs, American architects preferred to improve existing cities. The aspiration to improve the quality of life within the cities was accompanied by a conscious search for beauty and order. Its roots were both in public demand for healthier living, as well as in the strong desire of professionals to apply their knowledge to solve social problems.

As in Britain, in the latter part of the nineteenth century rapid and uncontrolled growth of cities resulted in a chaotic pattern of development. Urban populations expanded as developing industries offered new opportunities to immigrants from abroad as well as to citizens. Between 1870 and 1900 the population of the United States doubled, and by 1910 almost half of Americans lived in an urban area, compared to slightly more than one in four in 1880.[15] As demand for better conditions in the city grew, pressure increased on local governments to restrain socially harmful activities, to provide new services, and to take steps toward controlling the physical shape of the city. Interest among city governments to expand the scope of activities and accept more responsibilities resulted in annual conferences, as well as the formation of professional organizations.

Frederick Law Olmsted, in the closing years of the nineteenth century, advocated the creation of a formal organization for the advancement of planning and civic design. He saw in such an undertaking a way to create identity and pride among practitioners and to promote public education and government legislation. As a result of such efforts, the American Society of Municipal Improvement was formed in 1894, soon followed by the creation of the American Park and Outdoor Art Association (APOAA) in 1897.

Another catalyst for the movement for improvement and beautification of towns and cities was the World's Columbian Exposition in Chicago in 1893. The fair's vision of immense, white neoclassical buildings facing naturalistic landscapes and sparkling lagoons stood in shining contrast to the dark reality of typical city living. Even after its closing and demolition 6 months after opening, its image remained a powerful reminder and inspiration for many designers, artists, and architects who argued that city improvements would create civic pride, and that beautiful surroundings would enhance productivity and the urban economy. Although the main aim was to improve aesthetics through public buildings, civic centers, parks, and boulevard systems, advocates of the City Beautiful movement also included ordinary street improvements, good paving, street furnishings and planting in their agendas.

Among the noted people behind the movement for civic beautification were the president of the American League for Civic Improvement, J. Horace McFarland, architect Daniel Hudson Burnham, Frederick Law Olmsted, Jr., and Charles Mulford Robinson. Although Burnham is often thought of in connection with the City Beautiful era because of his spectacular design for the World's Columbian Exposition and his plans for San Francisco, Chicago, and Washington, D.C., it was Robinson who exerted much larger influence and offered an interesting contrast. Author of the best-selling book *The*

Improvement of Towns and Cities, first published in 1902,[16] Robinson was neither an architect nor a designer, but rather a journalist and a publicist who wrote several books and numerous magazine articles on the issue of civic design. He lectured at Harvard in 1911 and was the first Chair of Civic Design in the country at the University of Illinois in 1913. Unlike his architect counterparts who saw their major contribution as the design of major buildings and civic plazas, Robinson stressed the need for practical improvements in virtually all city planning spheres. He addressed the need for improving transportation, site planning, watercourses, playgrounds, street patterns and widths, paving, lighting, and sanitation. Robinson argued for natural beauty, parks, and the greening of the cities through street planting. Although an advocate for the creation of civic and town centers, he realized the importance of the local neighborhood. Towns, in his view, should be built as a series of neighborhoods centered around a focal point, such as schools, public buildings, or parks. This idea was later adopted and applied all over the country through the neighborhood unit principles promoted by Clarence Perry, the Regional Planning Association, and the federal government.

The City Beautiful movement is often criticized for being impractical, expensive, and aimed at pure beautification. Yet most of Robinson's suggestions dealt with practical issues of the city rather than issues of pure beauty. Streets, particularly small residential streets, were of particular concern to Robinson. He went so far as to publish a book on the subject in 1911: *The Width and Arrangement of Streets.* In it Robinson discusses the full spectrum of city street design, from general platting, width, and influence on land value, to the construction of curbs and gutters. He wrote: "Consideration of the width and arrangement of streets, far from being a

Charles Mulford Robinson (1869–1917), author of *The Improvement of Towns and Cities* in 1901, was a major figure in the development of city planning in the early twentieth century and was a leader in the City Beautiful movement. *(University of Illinois Archives)*

1808 - Fountain in the Circle, Northbrae, Berkeley, California.

City Beautiful designers emphasized the integration of sculpture, landscape design, and architecture in the creation of civic spaces that would uplift society and transmit the highest values, as in this traffic circle on Marin Avenue in Berkeley. *(The Bancroft Library, University of California at Berkeley)*

by-path of investigation, proves a broad highway. All the currents of life, all the grades of society, are intimately affected by the problems it includes. The joy and pain of urban existence, the comfort or hardship of it, its efficiency or failure are influenced by the wisdom or the thoughtlessness with which streets are platted."[17]

Robinson stresses the economics of street construction and mentions the burden that falls upon the citizens when excessive and ill-platted streets are constructed. He often cites European designers such as Stübben and Unwin, and offers prototypes for good residential streets. "The street planner," he

John Nolen (1869–1937), a landscape architect and city planner, designed civic improvements and subdivisions across the country in the City Beautiful style. *(courtesy of Virgina Tech Special Collection Archive)*

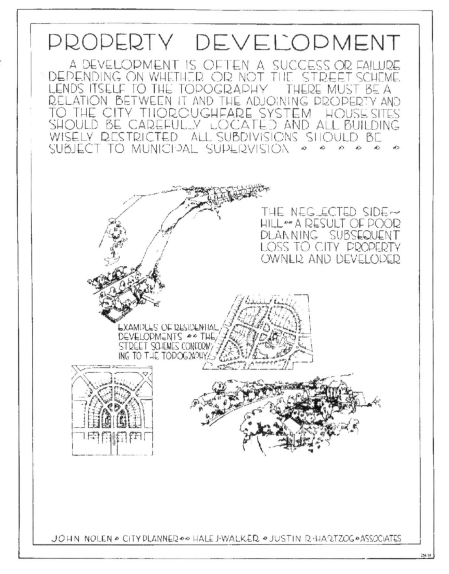

writes, "should approach the problem of the minor street with no predilection in favor of any geometrical system. With a perfectly open mind, he should simply seek the street layout that is most appropriate to the contours, that will most advantageously subdivide the property, and that will give the best connection and best shaped lots on the main highway. He should not approach this problem predisposed to adopt a gridiron, checker-board, or diagonal system."[18]

As to the width of minor residential streets, Robinson suggests the following proportion: "If the street be fifty feet or sixty feet wide they are perhaps most pleasantly of a breadth that brings the total distance from the curb to lot line up to one-half the width of the roadway, with the walk placed a foot from the property line. The proportions of sides and center space thus become 1: 2: 1. On a fifty-foot street, we thus have a twenty-five foot roadway, and six-foot margins for grass between the paved walk and the curb; on a sixty-foot street, we have, or could have, a thirty-foot roadway and nine-foot margins. Less roadway and more margin would of course look better."[19] Robinson continues by stressing the importance of economical construction through narrow roadways. He goes further to suggest the elimination of sidewalks and the sharing of the roadway by pedestrians and vehicles in lightly travel areas.

Robinson's visions of cities composed of neighborhoods focused on community centers and civic open spaces, of streets that are sensitively and economically laid out to provide "the channel of the common life" was adopted by many designers in the 1920s and 1930s. Unfortunately, his practical solutions to neighborhood planning have often been ignored by contemporary writers who credit his visions to those who followed him. His ideas were very progressive for the time and in some ways they parallel thinking today in Europe and elsewhere, as discussed later in this book.

Streets for the Motor Age

The Car and the Urban Scene

Restore human legs as a means of travel. Pedestrians rely on food for fuel and need no special parking facilities.

—Lewis Mumford (1895-1990)

From the middle of the nineteenth century, road development both in Europe and in the United States was held back by the push to expand railroads. Although road building technology advanced during this period, vehicle performance lagged largely because of governmental limitations and policy that favored rail and stage coaching. Steam vehicles appeared in England as early as 1769 and developed rapidly until 1866 when Parliament passed the "Red Flag Law." This inhibiting ordinance required self-propelled vehicles on public roads to be limited to a maximum speed of 4 miles an hour, carry a minimum of two people, and be accompanied by a third person on foot who carried a red flag to give warning and help control frightened horses.[1]

Deterioration of the road system first aroused public attention, surprisingly, because of the bicycle, a new and popular mode of travel. Invented in 1580, it reached its peak in 1877 with the introduction of a low rear-wheel-driven "safety" bicycle. The new bicycle captured the public imagination by offering convenience and mobility that was both safe and cheap. In the period from 1890 to 1895, often referred to as the "Bicycle Craze Era," bicycle

MOVEMENTS FOR ROAD AND STREET IMPROVEMENT

Steam vehicles first appeared in England in 1769. The Red Flag Law, passed by Parliament in 1866, restricted the rapid development of self-propelled vehicles by limiting the speed to four miles an hour. A person on foot with a red flag was required to give warning and to control frightened horses. *(U.S. Department of Transportation, Federal Highway Administration)*

53

In the mid-nineteenth century road development lagged, both in Britain and the United States, because government policy favored railroad expansion. *(California Dept. of Transportation)*

clubs in both England and the United States lobbied for road improvements. The League of American Wheelmen was formed in 1880 and it, too, constantly lobbied for road improvements.

These efforts brought recognition of the need for local road-aid laws; New Jersey adopted such laws in 1891, and in 1892 the National League for Good Roads was founded. The New Jersey state-aid road law stated: "The state-aid road law provides for the appointment of Township committees who should annually inspect the roads of their townships, and adopt a systematic plan for improving the highways; they should have power to employ an engineer or any competent person for advice, plans and estimates . . . it is estimated that at least 27,000 tons of water fall annually on one mile of road, and the necessity of a well-rounded road-bed, with open side ditches from outlet to outlet, is an important feature."[2] Public dissatisfaction with the condition of the roads resulted in many complaints and petitions to Congress. In 1893 one of the most influential of these petitions, signed by thousands including governors of many states, requested the creation of "a Road Department, similar to the Agriculture Department, for the purpose of promoting knowledge in the art of constructing and maintaining roads."[3] With this growing pressure the federal government established the Office of Road Inquiry within the Department of Agriculture in 1893: "To enable the Secretary of Agriculture to make inquiries in regard to the system of road management throughout the United States, to make investigations in regard to the best method of road making, to prepare publications on this subject suitable for distribution and to enable him to assist the agriculture college and experiment stations in disseminating information on this subject, ten thousand dollars ($10,000)."[4] These acts established a regular road inspec-

The poor condition of roads became a public concern in the late nineteenth century because of the surge of interest in the bicycle. *(U.S. Department of Transportation, Federal Highway Administration)*

The invention of the low-wheeled "safety" bicycle in 1877 helped make the bicycle popular because it was cheap and safe. These gentlemen recorded their entire bicycle journey from Berkeley to Lake Tahoe in photographs in 1899. *(Herbert Gayles Collection, The Bancroft Library, University of California at Berkeley)*

tion and improvement program carried out by local authorities as well as the federal government.

For almost 20 years, the activities of the office were purely educational. Only in 1913, after growing demands by motor vehicle users and with the passage of the Post Office Appropriation Act, did the Office of Public Roads engage in road construction that was for more than experimental purposes.

55

THE CAR IN THE
EARLY 1900S

Developed in Europe in the latter part of the nineteenth century, and introduced to the United States soon after, the motor vehicle was still a rare sight on the streets of American cities in the early 1900s. At that time there were only 8,000 privately owned motor vehicles registered in the United States, many of them propelled by steam. Gasoline was still a waste by-product of the manufacture of kerosene and only a few pioneers dared to experiment with it as a practical propulsion medium. Some of those pioneers' names became identified with their products as well as with the new industry to come. Among them, the names of Henry Ford, David Dunbar Buick, and the Dodge brothers, John and Horace, of Detroit; Ransom E. Olds (Reo) of Lansing, Michigan; the Studebaker brothers, Henry and Clem, of South Bend, Indiana, have survived to become legends, as well as the names of giant corporations of later years.[5]

The period from 1900 to 1929 saw the introduction of nearly 1,200 new automobile designs with various means of self-propulsion. This wave reached its peak in the year 1907 when 92 new entries appeared on the scene. In 1910, American factories made 181,000 passenger cars and 6,000 trucks and buses. The invention of the automobile self-starter, together with the shorter fashions in women's skirts, served to introduce women into the market: "The striking elevation of the lower hem of women's skirts began about 1910, in which year it advanced from about the knob of the ankle-bone upward as far as the shoe-top. In the same year, the automobile self-starter was perfected and put on the market. So long as automobiles had to be cranked by hand, it was taken for granted that women generally could not be drivers or owners. With electric self-starters came realization by automobile manufacturers that their market might be increased by persuading women they could now drive. When woman began to move her feet about among the pedals of a car, long skirts became an inconvenience."[6]

Other factors that helped the popularization of the car were affordable prices, the development of good roads, and safety devices that reduced the hazards of driving such as the demountable rim, the cord tire, four-wheel brakes, and light and signal devices.

The appearance of the motor vehicle on the American scene, like the bicycle, increased pressure for road improvements; the American Automobile Association was founded in 1902. A key development was the production of the model "T" Ford in 1907. A nationwide road census in 1904 showed 2,151,570 miles (3,442,512 km) of roads, of which only 7 percent were classified as "improved" or surfaced with stone or gravel. The remaining 93 percent were dirt roads. In 1900 there were only 8,000 motor vehicles using these roads, but by 1914 the production of motor vehicles exceeded the output of wagons. By 1920 there were 8 million vehicles.[7] The popularity of the automobile increased pressure on the government, and in 1916 Congress passed the Federal Aid Road Act, the first comprehensive government action to integrate the country's road system and establish a nationwide state highway system.[8]

During the early years of the motor vehicle, many argued that it posed a danger and a nuisance, and as such should be denied the use of the public streets. Although the general rule was to accept the equal rights of all to use the roads, laws regulating the operation and conduct of automobile drivers were soon established. Recognizing that the safety and welfare of those using horse-drawn equipment was seriously jeopardized by the danger of runaways upon seeing or hearing a motor vehicle, many regulations were introduced. Most of these laws, ordinances, and regulations enacted in the early years of the twentieth century were devised to limit the development of the automobile.

Among the numerous, often humorous, regulations, perhaps the wildest were drawn up by the Anti-Automobile Society, formed in Pennsylvania when the problem was first coming to the fore. There the farmers decided that anyone driving a horseless carriage at night should come to a stop every mile and send up a signal rocket, then wait 10 minutes for the road to clear. If a team of horses should approach along the road, the motorist was obliged to pull off the road and cover his vehicle with a large canvas or painted cloth that would blend with the surrounding landscape. If the horses refused to pass even then, the motorist had to take his vehicle apart piece by piece and hide the pieces under the nearest bush.[9]

Despite early resistance, by the 1930s the motor vehicle was in full control of the transportation scene. From 8,000 vehicles in 1900, to 23 million vehicles in 1930, the car had become a recognized and indispensable part of modern life. It immensely impacted the social, economic, and political structure of modern society. The car brought adventure for the average family, allowing new recreation and traveling opportunities. It allowed for the devel-

EARLY RESPONSES TO THE AUTOMOBILE

The automobile allowed the development of new suburbs away from city centers and rail transit. *(The Bancroft Library, University of California at Berkeley)*

57

opment of new suburban communities away from the city center and the railroad stations. The car virtually erased state lines, and brought demand for better roads. Better roads inspired manufacturers to build more speed and maneuverability into cars, which in turn demanded still higher road construction standards. Street layouts and road building became the essence of planning and development and a determining factor in shaping the pattern of the environment.

THE RISE OF COMPREHENSIVE PLANNING

At the turn of the century, as the automobile was beginning to appear on the urban scene, the American city was regarded as a chaotic environment of congestion and social unrest. Against it stood the ideal of a disciplined technological city with perfect spatial order. A new direction for civic improvement that ran counter to the City Beautiful was emerging that would reform the environment and discipline it through the use of expert knowledge, state regulatory mechanisms, and public welfare provisions. Reformers turned to science and technology as the means for change, with the premise that physical remedies could not only upgrade living conditions, but also resolve social problems. Experts were called on to recommend policies and administer scientific solutions. In his 1911 book *The Principles of Scientific Management*, Frederick Winslow Taylor, a pioneer in the efficiency movement, wrote: "The goal of human labor and thought is efficiency. Technical calculation is in all respects superior to human judgment, in fact human judgment cannot be trusted because it is plagued by laxity, ambiguity and unnecessary complexity. Subjectivity is an obstacle to clear thinking. . . . That which cannot be measured either does not exist or is of no value. . . . The affairs of citizens are best guided and conducted by experts."[10]

The principle of scientific management captured the minds of business, industry, and developers. It applied calculated conduct and insured profitability. Architects and planners soon followed. In the 1917 publication of *City Planning Progress* by the American Institute of Architects, the editors stated: "City planning in America has been retarded because the first emphasis has been given to the 'City Beautiful' instead of the 'City Practical.' We insist with vigor that all city planning should start on the foundation of economic practicableness and good business; that it must be something which will appeal to the businessman, and to the manufacturer, as sane and reasonable."[11] Intervention by guiding expert agencies was viewed as a practical tool to encourage change and promote the private sector. It was not seen as paternalism but as a "deliberate intention to use the government machinery for doing those things for which experience shows it to be more efficient and economical than any other means yet devised."[12]

At the turn-of-the-century, congestion, overcrowding, and unsanitary conditions of cities increased concerns for public health. Thus, tenements and slums were the first focus of many early planning remedies. The rise of scientific surveys and social statistics led Congress to authorize an investigation of slums in the cities in 1892. By 1900 more than 3,000 surveys had been produced, many of them by private organizations.[13] With the prevailing spirit of technology and science, rational planning and utilitarian ethics guided policy. The search for rationality inspired fresh approaches to planning, notably the adoption of the German concept of zoning and transportation systems, and the English comprehensive plan.

Pressure for professional solutions prompted the First National Conference on City Planning and the Problems of Congestion in 1909 in Washington, D.C. This was the first formal expression of interest in systematic solutions to the problems of America's urban environment. Remedies encouraged private enterprise to build at the edge of cities to relieve congestion. By redistributing the middle class to the outlying urban areas it was believed that pressures for housing would be relieved and lower-income people could obtain better housing. Theoretically, older housing was to serve as a ground for upward social mobility, while home ownership in new areas would establish social and economic stability. By advocating redistribution of the population into outlying areas, providing fast and low-cost transportation, and enticing industry to locate at the fringe, it was thought that city density would decrease. The conference attracted the attention of senators and representatives, and President Taft showed his interest by making the opening address. At this conference and those that followed, the groundwork for city planning structure and implementation techniques were formed. Issues such as "The Best Methods of Land Subdivision" and "Street Widths and Their Subdivision" provided the framework on which federal, state, and local governments established zoning and subdivision regulations at a later stage.

World War I gave planners and architects a chance to test their ideas with government backing. Starting in 1917 Congress apportioned $110 million to the Bureau of Industrial Housing to plan and construct housing and transportation needed for shipbuilding and armament centers. Under the direction of F. L. Olmsted, Jr., architects, landscape architects, planners, engineers, contractors, physicians, and social workers drew up a set of recommendations for war and postwar industrial housing. These recommendations aimed at producing self-sufficient neighborhood units fitted to the natural topography. They also provided guidelines and measurements for building arrangements.[14]

Decentralization of the American city got a major boost at the end of World War I. The war effort stimulated the economy and in order to keep it aloft there was a search for new investment which culminated in the formation of Better Homes in America, a network of developers and interest groups. The movement encouraged home ownership and spread the knowledge of financing for home purchases and home improvements. With the new construction cycle—the acquisition of land, the opening of new routes to the suburbs for the automobile, and the highway development program—a new metropolitan fringe based on speculative development began to take shape.

In 1914 the U.S. Housing Corporation formulated some of the first guidelines for residential streets. *(U.S. Department of Labor)*

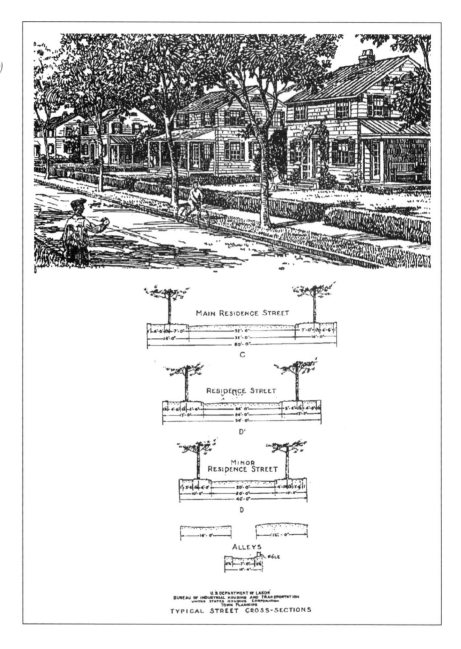

As city boundaries expanded unrestrained, planners sought ways to bridge the gaps between the city, the suburbs, and the open region. In 1923, twenty planners and architects, including Lewis Mumford, Henry Wright, Clarence Stein, Frederick Ackerman, Clarence Perry, and Stuart Chase, formed the Regional Planning Association of America (RPAA), hoping to develop guiding principles for designing more satisfying residential environments. Looking for a theory of metropolitan and regional planning, they

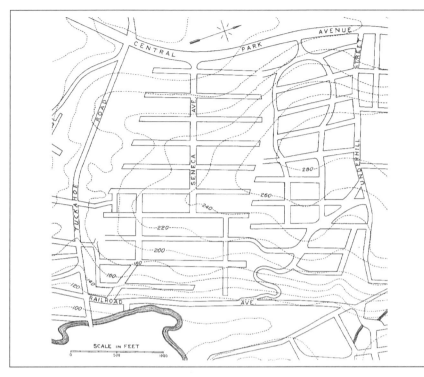

This 1914 subdivision layout from Yonkers, New York points out the need for planning. The grids ignore each other and make poor use of the site. The result is weak neighborhood structure and a circulation nightmare. *(Regional Plan of New York)*

The streetcar brought the first wave of suburbanization in U.S. cities. In cities throughout the country, new suburban developments grew up around streetcar lines. This view is of the Berkeley Heights district of Berkeley, California, about 1910. *(Mason McDuffie, The Bancroft Library, University of California at Berkeley)*

BERKELEY HIGHLANDS.

THE MOST ATTRACTIVE EXCLUSIVE RESIDENCE DISTRICT IN THE BAY CITIES, IS REACHED BY THIS, THE MOST DE-LIGHTFUL SCENIC DRIVE-WAY ON SAN FRANCISCO BAY. ADEQUATE BUILDING RESTRICTIONS INSURE HIGH-CLASS HOMES FOR CULTURED PEOPLE.

WRITE FOR BIRDS-EYE VIEW AND DESCRIPTIVE BOOKLET.

ARLINGTON AVENUE APPROACHING BERKELEY HIGHLANDS.

MEIKLE, BROCK & SKIDMORE, GENERAL AGENTS
ESTABLISHED 1892

2121 SHATTUCK AVE., BERKELEY, CAL.
LARGEST BERKELEY DEALERS

Clarence Stein, in collaboration with Henry Wright, interpreted the Garden City idea in the American context. His built work includes Sunnyside Gardens in Queens, New York; Radburn in Fairlawn, New Jersey; Chatham Village in Pittsburgh; Greenbelt, Maryland; Greendale, Wisconsin; Baldwin Hills Village in Los Angeles; and several other projects. *(Division of Rare and Manuscript Collections, Cornell University Library)*

adopted aspects of the Garden City model of Ebenezer Howard, advocating a regional pattern of economically related but autonomous urban units ringed by open space. Specifically, the group looked to Unwin and Parker's work for a new physical structure for the suburban environment.

In 1924 Clarence Stein and Henry Wright made a pilgrimage to England to study the design of Letchworth and Hampstead Garden Suburb, hoping to apply it to the American situation. They persuaded Raymond Unwin to help shape the theoretical framework of the group and thereafter he became actively involved in the American planning scene. Mumford, the historical and theoretical force behind the group, proclaimed: "Manifestly, the suburb is a public acknowledgment of the fact that congestion and bad housing and blank vistas and lack of recreational opportunity and endless subway rides are not humanly endurable. The suburbanite is merely an intelligent heretic who has discovered that the mass of New York or Chicago or Zenith is a mean environment."[15] Yet Mumford also acknowledged that existing suburbs needed reshaping and redesign in order to correspond to the new visions of residential communities. "The very forces that created the suburb moved out, inexorably, with icy relentlessness, and began to smear away this idyllic environment, which had the neighborliness of a small community and the beauty of gardens and parks and easy access to nature. Inevitably the suburb grew and, growing, it became more like the city it had only apparently broken away from: the market street lengthened into a garish main street . . . . Land values boomed; but taxes, alas! rose too . . . . All the costs of sewers, paving, unnecessarily wide residential streets, street lighting, gas, electricity, and police went up so rapidly that presently the newcomers could no longer afford a roomy, comfortable house like that which the Joneses had built: they put up monotonous semi-detached rows or plumped into apartments."[16]

STEIN, WRIGHT, AND RADBURN

The opportunity to test the Garden City model in America came in 1924 when Alexander M. Bing, a real estate developer and a charter member of the Regional Planning Association, founded the City Housing Corporation "for the ultimate purpose of building an American garden city."[17] The corporation's chief architects, Clarence Stein and Henry Wright, had designed Sunnyside Gardens in New York City, a small development of row houses— not a full scale Garden City. Yet its economic success provided the basis for a larger project, Radburn in Fairlawn, New Jersey, 16 miles (25.6 km) from New York City. The complete garden city of Radburn was planned in 1928 on 2 square miles (5.2 sq km) for a population of 25,000. Although the English Garden City model was the inspiration for their design, Stein and Wright realized that their project had to respond to American living conditions and the growing use of the automobile. Stein acknowledged that the Radburn plan was a reaction to the state of the city: "American cities were certainly not places of security in the twenties. The automobile was a disturbing menace to city life in the U.S.A.—long before it was in Europe . . . .

The Radburn plan, dating from 1928, builds on some ideas of the English Garden city. However, the sizes of both the superblocks and the green spaces in the center are much larger. All of the housing is situated on narrow, quiet cul-de-sacs that connect with the green spaces. The cul-de-sac arrangement reduced street area and the length of utility lines by 25 percent. The resulting cost savings paid for the parks. *(Division of Rare and Manuscript Collections, Cornell University Library)*

The flood of motors had already made the gridiron street pattern, which had formed the framework for urban real estate for over a century, as obsolete as a fortified town wall . . . . The checkerboard pattern made all the streets equally inviting to through traffic. Quiet and peaceful repose disappeared along with safety. Porches faced bedlams of motor throughways with blocked traffic, honking horns, noxious gases. Parked cars, hard gray roads and garages replaced gardens."[18] Radburn's design was a reaction against city traffic and the impact of cars on residential living and as such it had to "accept the role of a suburb" rather than that of a garden city.[19]

Aerial view of Radburn in 1929. Although it is situated in the midst of suburban Fairlawn, New Jersey, Radburn has good access to commuter rail lines to New York. *(Division of Rare and Manuscript Collections, Cornell University Library)*

None of the Radburn design features were completely new. Yet, as Stein acknowledged, their synthesis and integration into a comprehensive layout was a breakthrough in subdivision form. Superblocks with a green garden core had been used by Unwin in Letchworth and Hampstead Garden Suburb. At Radburn the superblocks were increased to between 30 and 50 acres (9.2 and 20 ha). They were aligned according to the topography and fewer units faced onto the main streets. The cul-de-sac was another adaptation from Hampstead Garden Suburb. Stein and Wright criticized the grid for its bias in favor of traffic, as well as its cost. They advocated the cul-de-sac as a rational escape from the limitations of the checkerboard plan, in which all streets are through streets, with the possibility of collisions between cars and pedestrians every 300 feet (91.5 m). The costs of through-street pavement and mainline utilities, they argued, were not fully understood, and they complained that realtors and municipal engineers had perpetuated obsolete forms. The Radburn cul-de-sac lane was designed at a 300- to 400-foot (91.5–122 m) length, with only a 30-foot (9.2 m) right-of-way, as opposed to the prevailing 50- to 60-foot (15.25–18.3 m) width. Stein further reduced the paved driving lane to 18 feet (5.5 m) and allowed for the 6-foot (1.8 m) utility strip on each side to be landscaped and thus visually part of the garden. Building setbacks were 15 feet (4.5 m), and provisions were made for on-street parking.

The Road System Hierarchy, the most innovative Radburn adaptation, was derived from Olmsted's route separation in New York's Central Park. Yet Stein and Wright went further than physically separating vehicles and pedestrians. They established a road hierarchy that for the first time was

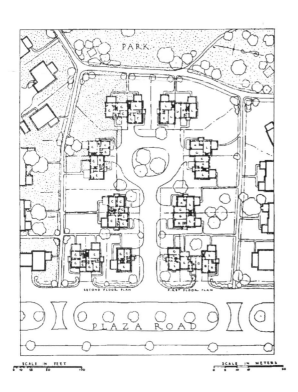

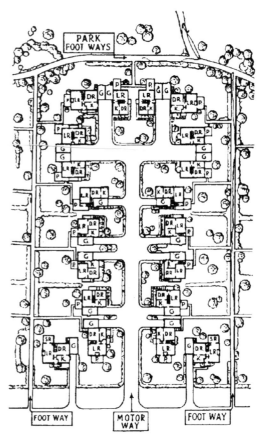

The Radburn lanes or cul-de-sacs are narrow with a 30-foot right-of-way. Houses have direct access to greenways that connect with the central parks. *(Division of Rare and Manuscript Collections, Cornell University Library)*

unchangeable and regulated—the layout permitted residential streets to be used only for local traffic. Stein said that the idea of purely residential streets was at that time "contrary to the fundamentals of American real estate gambling" and that "none of the realtors, and few city planners who accepted zoning as their practical religion, seemed to have faith enough in the permanency of purely residential use to plan streets to serve solely that use."[20] The Radburn superblocks were surrounded by 60-foot-wide (18.3 m) streets that served as feeders to the cul-de-sacs. The hierarchical layout allowed for considerable savings in road construction costs. As the cul-de-sac carried no through traffic, their standard of construction was less demanding. Curbs were not used, and sewer and water lines were smaller. Overall, the development was able to reduce street area and the length of utilities by 25 percent from what a typical gridiron street plan required. According to Stein, the cost savings for roads and public utilities, in comparison with the normal subdivision, paid for the construction of the main core parks.

Unfortunately, the Depression hit just as Radburn was being built, forcing the developer into bankruptcy. Thus, the project got off to a slow start and

Radburn cul-de-sac section.
(© Eran Ben-Joseph)

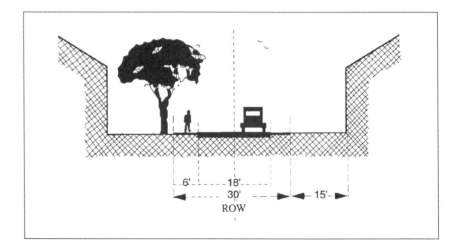

The Radburn cul-de-sacs provide automobile and service access to homes. Since they carry no through traffic, the standard of construction could be lower, with no curbs and smaller water and sewer lines.
(© Michael Southworth)

never had the impact it might have had. Although the plan was not fully realized, Radburn today is a very livable and attractive neighborhood that demonstrates the virtues of the Garden City concept. Surrounded by conventional gridiron speculative development, it is puzzling why Radburn did not become the model for the next decades. One answer may be that it is always more difficult to execute large-scale, integrated plans, when fragmented speculative development is an option. Also, the large amount of land devoted to public space represents a major cost to the developer, despite the savings in street construction costs. But perhaps more important, with the emphasis on shared public space, less land is devoted to individual yards than in conventional development; when given the choice of large public greens and

The pedestrian greenways are varied in landscape and architectural design. (© *Michael Southworth*)

Radburn's streets are structured in a hierarchy. The superblocks are served by 60-foot wide feeder streets. Pedestrian traffic is separated from vehicular traffic with grade separations at key points. (*Division of Rare and Manuscript Collections, Cornell University Library*)

Radburn's large central parks offer safe green spaces for children's play. (© *Michael Southworth*)

walkways versus large private yards, American home buyers have quite consistently chosen the latter.

The Radburn experience provided a new basis for residential planning and a new prototype for neighborhood layout based on a circulation hierarchy. With the influence of the car growing stronger, Radburn's structure exemplified the ideal for subdivision layout. As stated by Geddes Smith in 1929: "A town built to *live* in—today and tomorrow. A town 'for the motor age.' A town turned outside-in—without any backdoors. A town where roads and parks fit together like the fingers of your right and left hands. A town in which children need never dodge motor-trucks on their way to school. A *new* town—newer than the garden cities, and the first major innovation in town-planning since they were built."[21]

PERRY, ADAMS, AND THE NEIGHBORHOOD UNIT

A major issue addressed by the Regional Planning Association was the way in which uncontrolled and speculative regional growth diminished the sense of community in residential neighborhoods. As a member of both the Community Center Movement and the Regional Planning Association, Clarence Perry conceived "The Neighborhood Unit—A Scheme of Arrangement for a Family-Life Community."[22] Perry's concept was part of an extended process of regional planning for the New York area done between 1922 and 1929.[23] His aim was to find a fractional urban unit that would be self-sufficient yet related to the whole. He proposed six principles for the layout:

- *Size*: The residential unit should be determined according to the population that requires one elementary school: 750 to 1,500 families on a 150- to 300-net acre (62–120 ha) site with 40 percent of the area devoted to streets and open space.

- *Boundaries*: The unit should be bounded on all sides by arterial streets, sufficiently wide to eliminate through traffic in the neighborhood: 120-foot (36.6 m) right-of-way.

- *Internal Street System*: The unit should be designed with a hierarchical street system, each road proportioned for its probable traffic load to facilitate circulation within the unit but to discourage through traffic. Residential streets would have a 50-foot (15.25 m) right-of-way.

- *Open Spaces*: A system of small parks and recreation spaces should be provided.

- *Institutional Sites*: Sites for schools and other neighborhood institutions should be grouped at a central point.

- *Local Shops*: One or more shopping districts adequate to the population size should be placed at the edges of the unit, at traffic junctions, and adjacent to other neighborhoods.

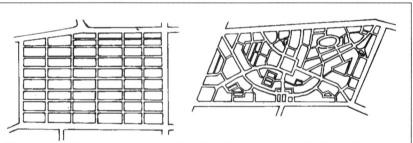

The proposed and the present neighborhood street systems. Left: Leading nowhere in particular. Right: Leading to the places where people go.

Clarence Perry conceived the neighborhood unit as focused on the elementary school, with no residence more than one-half mile from the school. Streets and pathways were to be designed to lead where people wanted to go, and through traffic was to be kept to the periphery. *(Division of Rare and Manuscript Collections, Cornell University Library)*

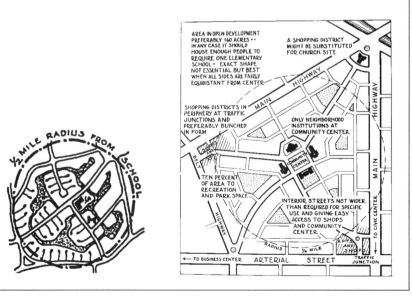

Perry's concepts were in tune with those of Raymond Unwin, who was regarded as an expert on neighborhood planning. Unwin's presentation to the New York Regional Committee in 1922 argued that increased transportation facilities would not cure congestion and that congestion was bound to be part of urban life. Thus, he argued, localities should protect neighborhood living through planning measures: fewer streets should be allowed to traverse residential areas; main streets should be located on viaducts bridging over cross-street traffic; and private automobile traffic should be relegated to specific routes away from transportation facilities.[24]

Perry advocated the revision of traffic concepts and standards for the residential unit, and according to Mumford, he was instrumental in many of the ideas incorporated in Radburn. Together with Thomas Adams, he devised a set of guiding principles for residential street systems in the New York region. Its main suggestions were:

- Streets should be adapted to the traffic load and type of use they would have.
- Street layout should fit the land, for attractiveness and lower cost.
- Main internal streets should be 60 to 80 feet (18.3–24.4 m) wide.
- Secondary streets should be from 30 to 60 feet (9.2–18.3 m) wide.
- For the local streets, a pavement width of 18 to 20 feet (5.5–6 m) is sufficient, and the balance of the right-of-way should be devoted to sidewalks and planting.
- There should be no street through the neighborhood in which the motorist can see a long stretch of uninterrupted road ahead.
- If a long straight street is unavoidable, landscape circles or ovals should be interposed at junctions in such a way as to compel cautious driving.
- Staggered cross streets, dead-end streets, and cul-de-sacs contribute to safety, attractiveness, and variety.
- Cul-de-sacs and dead-end streets should be used only as part of a complete subdivision plan integrating both pedestrian and vehicular circulation.
- If long blocks are used, pedestrian footpaths should offer shortcuts.[25]

The work of Perry and Adams contributed to the acceptance of the residential neighborhood as a unique entity that needed to be protected and deliberately planned. Although innovative and extensively published, the concept was not adopted by the private sector. The Federal Government endorsed it as early as 1932, but it was used only in large planning schemes such as the Greenbelt Town projects in the mid-1930s. Perry himself acknowledged that the chief obstacle to broader implementation of the concept was due to the prevailing small-scale building enterprises in the United States and the lack of comprehensive planning policies capable of implementing projects on a large scale.[26] Publication of Perry's work coincided with the economic catastrophe of 1929. With the collapse of the building industry, the lending and mortgage structure, and the halting of construction, a new planning structure was needed, one that would direct and control comprehensive policies through governmental authority.

While Wright and Unwin saw a solution to the social and physical ills of the city in the suburban Garden City, others believed the change should be carried out within the city itself. Perry's idea of a semi-independent walkable neighborhood cell that could be fit into any planning scheme offered a possible solution to the city's traffic ills. European Modernist architects found in this traffic-protected superblock the key to creating their ideal city. Architects and planners such as Le Corbusier, Walter Gropius, and Ludwig Hilberseimer viewed the automobile and technology as the forces that would shape this new city. Rejecting historical patterns, they conceived the city on a new scale that emphasized speed, movement, and efficiency, with a clear separation between pedestrians and the automobile. Le Corbusier called it the "machine-age revolution." A visionary scheme that could only be achieved with drastic changes to both planning practices and the actual form of the city, this visionary city for modern times was to be ruled by a preconceived plan designed by professionals.

The "machine-age revolution" was launched in the summer of 1928 with the first International Congress for Modern Architecture (CIAM) in Switzerland. The Congress, which attracted members of the European architectural and business worlds, established a "general program of action aiming to wrest architecture from the academic impasse and place it in its genuine economic and social setting."[27] Standardization, order, and control were the motto for economic success. Social and political reform were not far behind. Prefabricated, uniform dwellings, nested in planned cities would be the ultimate expression of an efficient society.

By the third congress in Brussels in 1933, CIAM tried to disassociate itself from the Garden City and the suburban ideal. Le Corbusier and his colleagues proclaimed that the Garden City leads to: "a sterile isolation of the individual" and the "annihilation of the collective will."[28] Their solution was in the city itself—a city made for speed and commercial success.

Le Corbusier admired the rectilinear grid cities of the United States, but was appalled by the medieval cities of Europe and Sitte's revival of picturesque aesthetics. For him, the modern city should be governed by the straight line for efficient traffic circulation and not by the "pack-donkey's way" of the old towns: "The circulation of traffic demands the straight line; it is the proper thing for the heart of the city. The curve is ruinous, difficult and dangerous; it is a paralyzing thing. . . . The winding road is the Pack-Donkey's way, the straight road is man's way. The winding road is the result of happy-go-lucky heedlessness, of looseness, lack of concentration and animality. The straight

European Modernism and the Vision for New Streets

road is a reaction, an action, a positive deed, the result of self-mastery. It is sane and noble."[29] "Let us adopt the curve if we want streets to walk in, little countrified walks, where there is no architecture, and the result will be a sort of small park or laid-out garden for promenaders and nursemaids."[30]

In their schemes the familiar city street framed by buildings and filled with diverse activities disappeared. A collection of towers, freestanding in a park-like setting, were to be served by a grid of elevated streets, 15 feet above ground (5 m) and 93 to 180 feet wide (28–54 m) crossing each other every quarter mile (about 400 m). The ground plane was to be occupied exclusively by pedestrians with no need to ever cross a street. Vehicular traffic, which was seen as detrimental to the quality of residential urban life, would be separated from the living environment. Le Corbusier exclaimed: "TO LIVE! To breathe—TO LIVE! Homes to inhabit. The present idea of the street must be abolished: DEATH OF THE STREET! DEATH OF THE STREET!"[31]

For the Modernists, the city was like a complicated machine, and therefore could function only on the basis of strict order. Thus, residents were to forget the pleasures of the picturesque or the accidental arrangement of a medieval village and embrace the efficiency and functionality of pure form. The results of this vision were often disasters: a City of Tomorrow with no human scale, without a fundamental understanding of human nature and social behavior, and with public streets that were no more than traffic channels. They ignored the fact that streets are places for community interaction, shopping, and cultural activity, and that cars are a part of daily urban life and thus should be integrated into the street design. Further, the Modernists ignored streets as the fundamental spatial structure for the built form of the city defined by the relationships between street widths and building height, between openness and enclosure, and sequence and separation.

Not all Modernists shared Le Corbusier's vision of elevated streets and high-rise buildings. Ludwig Hilberseimer and Mies van der Rohe, who made the United States their new home, were more receptive to Americans' aspirations for a suburban, low-density living style. Hilberseimer, who was teaching at the Illinois Institute of Technology along with Mies van der Rohe, conceived a new settlement pattern integrating community, industry, and agriculture. Building upon the ideals of standardization and functional hierarchy, these settlement units segregated the elements of a city according to their function: "On one side of the traffic artery lies the industrial area; on the other side, the buildings for commerce and administration, located within a green belt, and then the residential area surrounded by a park area in which schools, playgrounds, and community buildings are placed. Gardens and farms, meadows and forests adjoin this park area. All streets within such a unit are closed-end streets. Through traffic is thus avoided, and with it danger to pedestrians."[32]

Fortunately, the expression of Modernism was directed primarily toward buildings. The architects' utopia of the new city remained mainly an architectural fantasy. Even though the Modernist movement provided the basis

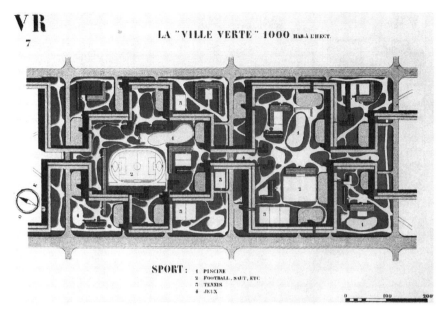

LA "VILLE VERTE" 1000 HAB. À L'HECT.

SPORT :
1 PISCINE
2 FOOTBALL, SAUT, ETC
3 TENNIS
4 JEUX

Le Corbusier and other Modernists conceived cities on a new scale. Streets were no longer settings for social activities. "The street is a traffic machine; it is in reality a sort of factory for producing speed traffic. The modern street is a new 'organ.' We must create a type of street which shall be as well equipped in its way as a factory." *(Le Corbusier, 1929, 131)*

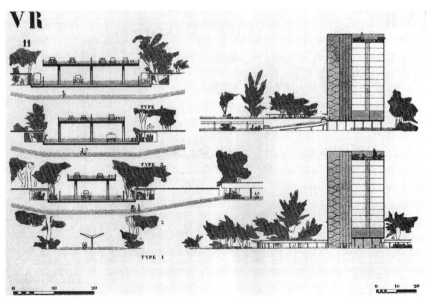

for the rebuilding of European cities after World War II, and some inner city renewal in the United States in the 1950s and 1960s, it did not take long for the public to realize the inherent flaws of the theory. Modern architecture claimed to be democratic, expressing the taste of the general public, but residents often saw the results as aloof and deceptive.

Many of the Modernists' ideas for making functional and efficient communities were in tune with American engineering approaches of the early

Ludwig Hilberseimer envisioned an efficient lower density city with a clear circulation hierarchy according to function and sharply separated land uses. All homes were to be on cul-de-sacs. Schools are placed in green space between residential districts. *(Hilberseimer)*

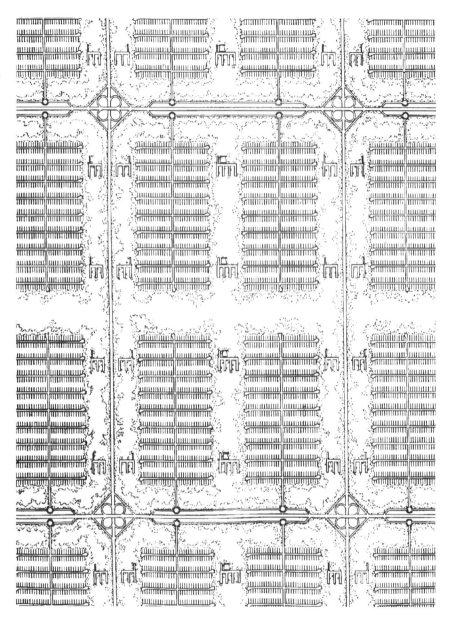

twentieth century, and have been implemented in the postindustrial American city through street design standards. In his vision for the Radiant City, Le Corbusier adopted street intersections directly from the New Jersey State Highway System, calling them "a perfect solution." He further explained: "Traffic is a river; traffic can be thought of as obeying the same laws as rivers do."[33] Similarly, Hilberseimer's hierarchical street system resembles transportation engineering standards of the 1970s and 1980s.

Following World War I, the 2 million motor vehicles of 1915 grew to almost 10 million by 1920, all attempting to use an inadequate road system. The impact of the automobile necessitated a comprehensive rethinking of transportation network policy in the United States. Although states were expanding their road systems, a coherent national road network had yet to be developed, one that would be coordinated financially and technically. This could only be achieved through federal action. In 1921 the Federal Highway Act provided federal aid to construct "such projects as will expedite the completion of an adequate and connected system of highways, interstate in character."[34] The Act was the first recognition in American transportation policy of a functional specialization for motor vehicle routes with control by a central authority. It provided the basis for a hierarchical road system and the first official categorization of roads and streets, in particular the separation of arterial through-traffic networks from local ones. Federal monetary aid generated the largest road improvement program in the nation. During the Depression years in particular, federal aid was extended to include urban and rural road systems. By 1938, road and street improvements reached a total of 600,000 miles (960,000 km), of which only 80,000 miles (128,000 km) were for highways.[35]

The change in transportation policy and the improvement of road systems demanded a new profession. In the first quarter of the century traffic engineering was not a recognized discipline and was not part of an established practice. In fact, between 1920 and 1930 it was not even recognized as a specialty within the American Society of Civil Engineers.[36] Road designers in the 1920s had to work within an emerging field of knowledge that developed through actual application. Except among a few engineers there was little knowledge of the fundamental differences between road construction techniques and transportation planning. Many of these early professionals were civil or electrical engineers who were self-taught in transportation planning and construction.[37]

Rapid changes in transportation prompted the formation of a professional specialty in transportation engineering in 1930 through the national Institute of Transportation Engineers (ITE) and a specialized program at Yale University. The new profession was defined as: ". . . a branch of engineering which is devoted to the study and improvement of the traffic performance of road networks and terminals. Its purpose is to achieve efficient, free, and rapid flow of traffic; yet, at the same time, to prevent traffic accidents and casualties. Its procedures are based on scientific and engineering disciplines. Its methods include regulation and control, on one hand, and planning and geometric design, on the other."[38] In 1939, the federal government, the National Conservation Bureau, and the American Association of Highway Officials asked ITE to suggest traffic engineering guidelines and standards for an engineering handbook and related technical publications. The first *Traffic Engineering Handbook* was published in 1942, providing the basis for professional practice.

Most of these early publications were concerned with efficient high-speed road networks, rather than local residential networks. In the 1940s, recommended lane widths and cross sections emphasized driver comfort and safety at high speeds. Traffic engineers expected wider lanes and cross sections would promote safety and efficient movement. A lane width of 12 feet (3.6 m) was usually recommended for mixed truck and passenger vehicles, and 11 feet (3.3 m) for passenger cars. Street parking lanes on urban streets were recommended to be 13 to 15 feet (4–4.5 m). The justification often given for these dimensions was: "The important factor in the width of parking lanes is the effect of the parked cars upon the capacity of the highway. A further reason for this width was the possibility that at some future time parking may be prohibited and the lane will become a through traffic lane. Wider parking lanes also decrease the interference with through traffic when vehicles are parking and unparking."[39]

Today the road and transportation engineering professions dominate development, but the underpinnings of the Modernist vision, although rejected by the public, survive in engineering models based on efficiency and movement.

Bureaucracy Takes Control

The Institutionalization of Standards

> *Standards are of the nature of habit. And habit is an outstanding characteristic of human action.*
>
> —National Industrial Conference Board, 1929

With the rise of government and professional bureaucracies in the 1930s came the institutionalization of many standards that continue to shape suburban form today. The harsh realities of the economic depression in the 1930s rendered American municipal authorities helpless. As local revenues fell and unemployment rates soared, many municipalities approached bankruptcy. When angry crowds of unemployed workers turned their frustration toward the local government, alarmed mayors and city officials turned in desperation toward the federal government. At the National Conference of Mayors in June of 1932, 29 cities sent a plea for help to the federal government. However, with the national election at stake, the Hoover administration was reluctant to increase direct help for cities and called a special President's Conference on Home Building and Home Ownership. The conference did not directly intervene or allocate any direct funding, but the proposals put forward there shaped the future of government intervention in housing. More than 3,700 experts on various aspects of home finance, taxation, and planning of residential districts formed committees and offered recommendations:

- To pass state-enabling acts granting city planning powers to municipalities
- To give priority to housing
- To follow the Neighborhood Unit principles in designing residential areas
- To adopt a set of subdivision regulations to control the design of new areas
- To adopt comprehensive zoning plans for cities, urban regions, towns, and counties
- To develop comprehensive mass transportation plans
- To preserve and develop an open space system in residential neighborhoods

The President's Conference findings were not directly implemented by the Hoover administration. With the election in sight it was left for the new

THE PRESIDENT'S CONFERENCE ON HOME BUILDING AND HOME OWNERSHIP

Democratic administration to adopt and integrate the conference recommendations into its policy. The new administration embraced its planning outlook and most of the recommendations of the conference experts. For the next decade planning discourse and its physical outcome were shaped by three major federal actions: the adoption of the 1932 President's Conference recommendations, the establishment of the National Planning Board in 1933 under the authority of the Public Works Department, and the establishment of the Resettlement Administration and the Federal Housing Administration (FHA) as part of the National Housing Act in 1934–1935.

The most influential recommendations of the Conference came from the Committees on City Planning and Zoning, Subdivision Layout, and Home Finance and Taxation. The Committee on Finance suggested that private enterprise acting alone could not guarantee successful affordable housing. Private enterprise, it felt, would gear itself to the upper income market share, and only through cooperation between government and the business sector could large-scale affordable housing be guaranteed. They encouraged the establishment of a federal regulatory procedure to aid the building industry with financial information on available mortgages, real estate transfers, and newly planned subdivisions. They also recommended the creation of a system of home mortgage discount banks to make home mortgage money more readily available and to encourage sound home financing practices. This proposal led to the Federal Home Loan Bank Act of 1932 and formed the basis for the FHA financial policies.[1] The Subcommittees on City Planning and Zoning asserted that the success of large-scale decentralized development could be achieved only through a new outlook on regional planning and a readjustment and restructuring of laws, codes, and standards. They recommended giving more power to city planning and other local officials. Endorsing the neighborhood unit concept, they recommended its usage in new planning, as well as in the restructuring of existing neighborhoods through zoning and regulations. The Committee on Subdivision Layout wanted to control speculative developers and proposed the adoption of good subdivision engineering and design and the enforcement of minimum standards to eliminate destabilizing practices.[2]

The recommendations of the Committee on Subdivision Layout were based on the principles of Perry's *The Neighborhood Unit*,[3] Thomas Adams's manuscript for *Residential Development*,[4] and the previous National Conferences on City Planning (especially the seventh, in 1915): "There should be a differentiation in the width and arrangement of streets. Main thoroughfares should be established not only for the accommodation of a large volume of traffic, but also to lessen the traffic on minor streets where the majority of dwellings will be located. As an added inducer of privacy and safety, minor streets should be of less width. Minor streets should also be designed with a certain curvature or indirectness so as further to discourage traffic and at the same time, to produce a departure from the usually monotonous rectangular pattern."[5]

The committee recommended that several aspects of streets be regulated:

- Relation of proposed streets to adjoining street systems
- Street alignment
- Street intersections
- Corner radii
- Dead-end streets
- Street right-of-way (easement): minimum 60 feet (18.3 m)
- Roadway width: 24 feet (7.3 m) minimum width 4 to 6 foot (1.2–1.8 m) sidewalk
- Building lines
- Street grades
- Street names
- Street trees (species list given)
- Block length, width, and area: maximum length 1000 feet (305 m)
- Lot lines: minimum of 15-foot (4.5 m) side yard between houses

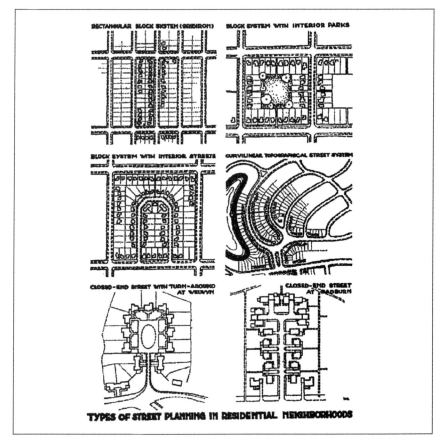

TYPES OF STREET PLANNING IN RESIDENTIAL NEIGHBORHOODS

The 1932 President's Conference recommended regulations for street design and layout to control speculative developers. They endorsed the neighborhood unit concept and based their recommendations on the work of Perry and Adams, as well as Unwin, Stein, and Wright. (*President's Conference on Home Building and Home Ownership, 1932*)

FHA development standards and mortgage assistance were the foundation for the suburbanization of U.S. cities. The standards supported established builders and put the 1920s "curbstone subdividers" and "Jerry-builders" out of business. *(Mason McDuffie, The Bancroft Library, University of California at Berkeley)*

ADOPTION OF NEIGHBORHOOD UNIT AND GARDEN CITY PRINCIPLES

In 1933 the Public Works Administration established the National Planning Board by executive order. This new advisory planning body adopted most of the President's Conference findings, as well as the philosophies of the Regional Planning Association and the design remedies suggested by its members. It endorsed the notion that urban decentralization could act as a catalyst for economic recovery, as long as it was controlled and not speculative in nature. For the structure of the community, it recommended the Neighborhood Unit and the Garden City ideals to support healthy and stable forms of living. Promoting the idea of coordinated planning, the National Planning Board encouraged the preparation of comprehensive regional plans through the cooperation of city, regional, and state agencies. The National Planning Board gained support from social activists and from President Roosevelt. Roosevelt was known to have antiurban views and often stated that economic stability could be achieved by moving away from an emphasis on the city and developing a regional structure: "The question we need to exercise is whether we cannot plan for a better distribution of our population as between the larger city and the smaller country communities. . . . Conditions have changed since the rush of workers to the cities began. They have changed materially even since the war period. One of the most significant transformations is that wrought by the automobile, and the improvement in highways that has come along as a consequence. . . . It is no longer necessary that an industrial worker should live in the shadow of the factory in which he works . . . the worker should have a wide range of choices for his home in terms of physical distance."[6]

Social scholars pointed out the uneven distribution of class between the suburbs and the city and concluded that rapid development catered to the upper class, causing deterioration of the social fabric of the city. They also attributed the slump in land values to the fact that developers were catering to a limited market. The 1933 Report of the President's Research Committee on Social Trends indicated that "special attention has been given in the past decade to the promotion of exclusive residential districts designed for occupancy by the higher income class. The lure of the rural scenery is indicated by the extremely high rates of increase of suburbs bearing names denoting attractive physical features, such as heights, vistas, parks, and water frontage. Here are some well-known suburbs with their percentage increase from 1920 to 1930: Beverly Hills, 2,485.9%; Glendale, 363.5%; Inglewood, 492.8% . . . Cleveland Heights, 234.4%; Shaker Heights, 1,000.4%; Garfield Heights, 511.3%."[7]

In 1934 the National Housing Act was passed to implement the recommendations of the various commissions and agencies. The Resettlement Administration and its Suburban Division were established in 1935 to promote new regional residential development amalgamating the three basic concepts of the Garden City, the Radburn approach, and the Neighborhood Unit into the Greenbelt New Town projects. Their official purpose was: (1) to give useful work to men on unemployment relief; (2) to demonstrate in practice the soundness of planning and operating towns according to certain Garden City principles; and (3) to provide low-rent housing in healthful surroundings, both physical and social, for families in the low-income bracket.

The Greenbelt New Town projects, however, never became an influential force in the American urban landscape. Only three towns were constructed and all of them failed to develop as centers of industry, business, or government, but became specialized suburban communities instead. Yet the planning philosophies behind their development strengthened the emphasis on the need for dwellings for low and moderate income groups in multifamily units as well as single family residential developments.[8]

As a result of the continued emphasis by the government on multilateral coordinated planning many local governments established regional plans to guide the growth of their communities. In the Northeast, for example, more than twenty regions had produced plans between 1932 and 1935. It was a major undertaking to provide a "framework to which all future detailed plans of various localities can be made to conform."[9] It was also an effort to coordinate suburban subdivision development through the integration of road planning and road standards and to prevent inappropriate street layouts. An official plan and an established guidelines map were seen as new tools to control and maintain governing policies. Thus, "the more common evils attended upon land subdivision: premature development, resulting in idle land, economic loss, and unsightly blots on the landscape; subdivision of land unsuitable for building; failure to adapt the street plan to the topography of the land; misfit subdivisions, that is, failure to co-ordinate the streets of adjoining tracts; failure to adapt street widths to their uses (too narrow

STREET REGULATIONS TAKE ROOT

thoroughfares and too wide residential streets); failure to set aside adequate spaces for play and recreation" could be eliminated through regional planning and coordination.[10]

Large scale planning efforts and integrated governmental policies resulted in a new planning and design structure. For the first time an inclusive outlook of planning was considered for both region and nation. Such a structure also demanded a centralized apparatus to coordinate and control the emerging landscape.

THE FEDERAL HOUSING ADMINISTRATION PROMOTES SUBURBANIZATION

Although the federal government encouraged long-range housing policies through professional planning discourse, it was its financial mechanism that shaped the new built environment. The FHA was established in 1934 as part of the National Housing act to restructure the collapsed private home financing system through government mortgage insurance plans. By providing a governmental protective shield, the FHA was able to eliminate the risk for lenders, as well as to provide a financial resource for home buyers. Developers benefited from new stimuli for existing project sales as well as incentives for new construction. Through its long-term, low-interest rates and low down payments a larger portion of the population found itself eligible and secure in buying a home.

FHA financial assistance and mortgage insurance was the foundation for the most ambitious suburbanization plan in U.S. history. A comprehensive system of appraisal procedures secured its investments against risk. In order to qualify for a loan, lenders, borrowers, and developers had to submit detailed plans and documentation of their projects to the administration to determine whether or not they had sound prospects. The FHA underwriting criteria soon became the prevailing standard. With monetary support at stake, developers preferred to comply with the published standards. Thus, FHA officials found themselves in a powerful position, far greater than any planning agency, to shape development for generations to come. In 1934 nearly 4,000 financial institutions, representing more than 70 percent of the nation's commercial banks, had FHA insurance plans. By 1959, FHA mortgage insurance had helped 5 million families (three out of every five) to purchase a home and helped to repair or improve 22 million properties.[11]

FHA's successful control over development and developers was not only due to their financial power, but also to the fact that they were not a pure planning agency. Community developers and the National Association of Real Estate Boards were enthusiastic about the FHA role, in contrast to their fear of government and local planning commissions.[12] The FHA, unlike other planning agencies, was largely run by representatives of real estate and banking industries, so developers felt that its intervention protected their interests. Establishing standards and underwriting also supported established builders, enabling them to further expand and construct large-scale residential subdivisions with government backing, putting the 1920s speculative style "curbstone subdividers" and "Jerry-builders" out of business. The paradox of the FHA system was that although it imposed strict requirements through underwriting manuals and property standards "it always appeared to be non-coercive to the private sector. The FHA was generally perceived as engaging in a simple business operation—to insure only low-risk mortgages with a sound economic future. Property owners and real estate entrepreneurs viewed FHA rules and regulations as similar to deed restrictions—private contracts which were freely entered into by willing parties—rather than as similar to zoning laws, which were sometimes seen as infringing on constitutional liberties."[13]

In January 1935, the FHA's first publication of technical standards appeared in five circulars: *Standards for the Insurance of Mortgages on Properties Located in Undeveloped Subdivisions—Title II of the National Housing Act.* In *Subdivision Development*, which was the basis for further publications by the Technical Division, the FHA stated that its general goals for successful development avoided setting any rules or procedures: "The Administration does not propose to regulate subdividing throughout the country, nor to set up stereotype patterns of land development."[14] Yet it goes on to endorse principles: "It does, however, insist upon the observance of rational principles of development in those areas in which insured mortgages are desired, principles which have been proved by experience and which apply with equal force to neighborhoods for wage earners as they do to those for the higher income groups." These rational principles are then described in detail, with precise measurements, in "Minimum Requirements & Desirable Standards." These standards laid the groundwork for the postwar suburban street pattern:

FHA'S FIRST STANDARDS

- The subdivision layout should fit the topography of the site and take advantage of natural features.
- Streets should be planned as to width and construction to suit the local requirements.
- Not all streets should be designed for through or heavy traffic.
- Paving for streets bearing purely local traffic may be of inexpensive materials and may, depending on the character of the neighborhood, omit curbs and sidewalks.
- Width of paving should be based on allowance of 10 feet (3 m) for each traffic lane and 8 feet (2.4 m) for each parallel parking line.
- All street intersections should be built on a radius of at least 20 feet (6 m).
- Long-lived, hardy trees should be planted along all streets.
- Blocks should generally range from 600 to 1000 feet (183–305 m) in length.
- A desirable lot for detached dwellings should be at least 50 feet (15.25 m) wide, with an area of no less than 6,000 square feet (540 sq m). For semidetached dwellings density should not exceed 12 units per acre (0.4 ha).[15]

STANDARDS ESTABLISH THE CUL-DE-SAC PATTERN

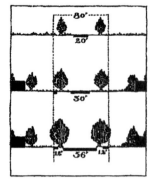

FHA's first publication in 1936 of a recommended street width illustrates the way in which street improvements on an 80-foot right-of-way could be gradually increased as the neighborhood grows. *(Federal Housing Administration)*

Having set the framework for regulation through written standards, the FHA provided additional suggestions and recommendations for development layout. The 1936 Bulletin on *Planning Neighborhoods for Small Houses* demonstrated the FHA preference for the town and neighborhood planning concepts of Unwin, Perry, and Stein.[16] Using plans and diagrams, some of which appeared in publications by Unwin and Perry, the bulletin illustrated how to build an ideal "well-balanced, carefully planned subdivision" that would also add up to "the creation of real estate values through devising a layout which is not only economically sound but which provides to the maximum degree those conditions which make for pleasant and healthful living."

Regarding overall subdivision layout, for the first time the FHA rejected the grid pattern for residential neighborhoods, a policy that continued in all of its subsequent publications. Using Perry's concept, the bulletin declared: "The gridiron plan which has been so universally adopted in most of our cities has several very decided disadvantages when applied to residential areas. In the first place it creates waste by providing a greater paved area than necessarily adequate to serve a residential community. Secondly, it causes the installation of a more expensive type of paving by dispersing the traffic equally through the area, which in turn creates an increased traffic hazard. In addition to these disadvantages it creates a monotonous uninteresting architectural effect and fails to create a community aspect."[17] A hierarchical structure was recommended for street layout. Major thoroughfares that provide access to centers were to be located along the borders and minor residential streets were within the development. Initiating a regular format, the bulletin used diagrams and section drawings to establish enduring standards for streets and lots.

Three forms of residential street layouts were put forward: curvilinear, cul-de-sacs, and courts. Their design was guided by descriptive and prescriptive standards:

- Layouts should discourage through-traffic;
- Wide intersections should be eliminated;
- Streets should follow the topography to reduce cost, create interesting vistas, and eliminate the monotony of long straight rows of houses;
- Minimum width of a residential street should be 50 feet (15.25 m), with 24-foot (7.3 m) pavement, 8-foot (2.4 m) planting/utility strips, and 4-foot (1.2 m) walks;
- Cul-de-sacs are the most attractive street layout for family dwellings; street construction costs are thereby reduced since an 18 foot (5.5 m) pavement with a minimum 30-foot (9.2 m) radius turnaround are sufficient;
- Setbacks for houses should be 15 feet (4.5 m) minimum;
- Permanent trees should be planted 40 feet (12.2 m) apart on both sides of the street, either halfway between the sidewalk and the curb, or on the outer side of the sidewalk and the property line;

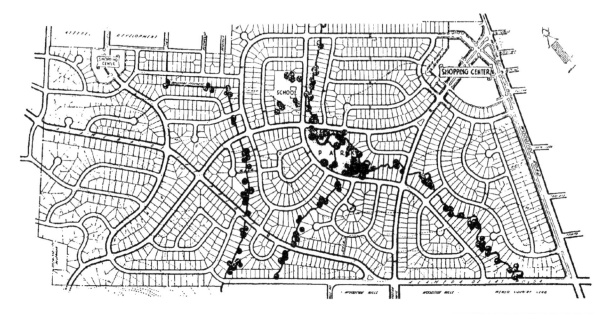

Woodside Acres, Redwood City, California, 1944. Using Perry's neighborhood unit concept, FHA rejected the gridiron pattern because of its cost, traffic hazards, and monotony. Shops are located on the edges along arterials, while the school and park are centrally placed within the district. Local residential streets are usually curving, and loops and cul-de-sacs are plentiful. *(Federal Housing Administration)*

- Front yards should avoid excessive planting for a more pleasing and unified effect along the street.

Subsequent publications by the FHA adhered to the established standards of 1936 and 1937, with no changes in street layouts or widths until 1941, when the minimum width of residential street pavement was increased from 24 feet to 26 feet (7.3-8 m), and concrete curb construction was recommended. Three types of concrete curbs were suggested: (1) a 12-in.-high (30 cm) battered curb, (2) a 12-in.-high (30 cm) curb and gutter, (3) a 12-in.-high (30 cm) rolled curb and gutter. In 1938 the FHA Technical and Land Planning divisions initiated a free review program for prospective developers who could submit preliminary plans for examination. Most FHA publications included the review procedure and required forms: "The FHA is interested in cooperating with real estate developers, builders, and their technical consultants in obtaining high standards of land development. The opportunity is welcomed to analyze proposed subdivisions and to make suggestions which, in our opinion, if followed, will create more marketable, attractive, and stable residential properties." FHA consultants would then analyze plans and suggest layouts conforming to FHA guidelines for securing an insured mortgage. It was a powerful control tool and naturally, almost all subdivision developers submitted their plans for review to ensure a guaranteed mortgage.

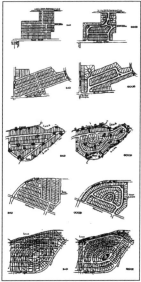

FHA's recommended subdivision layouts and minimum standards set the groundwork for modern subdivision design. All of the "bad" examples are based on the gridiron, while the "good" examples are based on the loop and cul-de-sac system. *(Federal Housing Administration)*

With the growth in automobile
ownership, more and more space
has been allocated to residential
streets. The standards are often
excessive, considering the low level
of traffic and slow speeds of local
streets. *(Mason McDuffie, The
Bancroft Library, University of
California at Berkeley)*

Lakewood, California, 1951.
Beginning in the 1950s vast areas of
new housing were built following
the FHA standards.
(© William Garnett)

Thus, the federal government was able to exercise tremendous power through the simple act of making an offer that could not be refused. The FHA was well aware of the implications of its authority. In 1935 FHA administrator James Moffett told his advisory board in a confidential meeting to "make it conditional that these mortgages must be insured under the Housing Act, and through that we could control over-building insertions, which would undermine values, or through political pull, building in isolated spots, where it was not a good investment. You could also control the population trend, the neighborhood standards, and material and everything

Many young families sought the suburban dream in the housing boom following World War II. New suburbs like Lakewood and Levittown spread across the country. *(J.R. Eyerman, Life Magazine, © Time Inc.)*

else through the president."[18] FHA minimum standards and design regulations had set the ground rules for modern subdivision development, which shaped the wartime housing projects of the Federal Public Housing Authority and provided the basis for the post–World War II suburbanization drive; these standards were also the foundation for local government subdivision regulations.

CONTROLLING SUBDIVISION THROUGH LOCAL PLAT APPROVAL

By 1941 thirty-two states had passed legislation granting the power of subdivision control to locally elected planning commissions. Through this exercise of legislative "police power" by the state, the right of a landowner to sell property became subject to approval by an authority designated to "promote the community health, safety, morals, and general welfare."[19] Local planning commissions, once authorized and empowered by the community, adopted rules and regulations governing subdivision procedures largely based on federal criteria, in particular those of the FHA. A nationwide survey of more than two hundred cities' requirements by the Public Administration Service in 1941 found them to be similar. The majority of cities established the functions of minor subdivision streets as providing access, light, and air to abutting property. All required proposed subdivision streets to conform with the street plan of the community, particularly for major streets, and encouraged discontinuity and the elimination of through traffic, as well.

An interesting shift had occurred with regard to dead-end streets. Early in the century developers often constructed dead-end streets with no regard to overall circulation planning, thus creating problematic street configurations; in the 1940s, however, properly designed dead-end streets were seen as desirable home locations.

The 1941 survey found that the width of minor streets and dead-end streets varied from 22 to 40 feet (6.7–12.2 m) for roadway width and from 50 to 60 feet (15.25–18.3 m) for right-of-way. Prevailing minimum widths for planting strips was recommended at 6 feet (1.8 m), for sidewalk width 4 feet (1.2 m), and for curb radii 20 to 25 feet (6–7.6 m). Of the 213 cities surveyed, 160 required a right-of-way of 50 to 60 feet (15.25–18.3 m); two cities—North Adams, Massachusetts and Bronxville, New York—required only 33 feet (10 m); and one city—Great Falls, Montana—80 feet (24.4 m). Traffic lane widths for minor streets were generally recommended at 9 feet (2.7 m), and parking lanes at 7 feet (2.1 m) as a minimum. Most regulations dealing with sidewalks set no definite rules but required the approval of the planning authority. The 4-foot (1.2 m) sidewalk was recommended for outlying residential streets, but not necessarily for the inner ones. In contrast to earlier practice, during the late 1930s and early 1940s almost all cities required that any street trees be planted on the property side of sidewalks: "While it has been customary in the past to plant street trees between the street curb and the pedestrian walk, an alternate procedure is now recommended as preferable in some cases. Trees planted along the street curb increases the severity of motor accidents and in turn are easily subjected to traffic injury; they interfere with and are injured by telephone wires and other utilities, the limited soil and water supply at the pavement edge restrain the tree growth and add replacement costs; and except on very wide streets, curb planted trees crowd in upon the traveled way. To plant street trees on the property side of pedestrian walks, away from the pavement and traffic, seems more desirable, particularly on residential streets."[20]

Subdivision regulations as exercised by a local planning agency were effective in implementing the community master plan. One might expect that in each locality, unique guidelines appropriate to its character would be developed. Indeed, local planning policies often stated as much: "Good subdivision design cannot be standardized and applied universally to all tracts, but only basic principles and minimum standards of design can be formulated."[21] In the design of residential streets diversity and freedom of choice were advocated: "In the development of residential neighborhoods, whether for the rich or for the poor, we usually need, in short, to get away from the stereotyped and formal. Our main traffic lines have freed our minor streets from the rules, restrictions, and system which traffic imposes on our main traffic thoroughfares; and the regulations determining the space which must be left open between the fronts of the opposite houses has given us the liberty to leave as much of this space in private, and as little in public ownership as may be convenient. We can have a sidewalk or omit a sidewalk, just as is best fitted to the conditions of the particular street; we can have a footway instead of a street if we prefer, or a road without a footway if that is better."[22] However, achieving diversity and adaptation to local conditions have often remained theoretical. The gap between a general principle and a local standard has not been bridged. Thus, most local agencies have ended up adopting the nationally prevailing set of subdivision standards put forward by the FHA.

THE INFLUENCE OF THE BUILDING INDUSTRY ON STREET DESIGN

The building industry, which supported a comprehensive national set of regulations such as the FHA standards, clearly was apprehensive about local agencies' guidelines, viewing them as unpredictable, hard to plan for, costlier, and less supportive of development. To help counter them and also to help home builders and the real estate community, several private organizations were formed, the most influential of which was the Urban Land Institute (ULI). Organized in 1939 as an independent nonprofit research organization in urban planning and land development, ULI was sponsored by the National Association of Real Estate and was a consultant to the National Association of Home Builders. The information it provided to developers and home builders about community development advocated the FHA approach to subdivision layout and adopted many of its recommendations. It tried to deter unconventional approaches to subdivision: "The ultra-modernist and the seeker for radical unorthodox, or socialized departures in this field will not find them here. What he will find will be considered recommendations of methods and procedures which have stood the test of sound land planning and engineering design, of the financial risks involved, and, most important, ideas which have the acceptance of the American home-buying public which is traditionally moderate in its selection of a home."[23] ULI publications pointed to inconsistencies in local agency requirements and often urged

The neighborhood unit principles are clearly seen in many subdivisions of the 1950s and later. *(© Pacific Aerial Surveys)*

The Urban Land Institute recommended a subdivision layout in 1947 that followed Perry's neighborhood unit principles. *(Urban Land Institute)*

modifications to facilitate construction and reduce costs. Thus, ULI has often acted as a catalyst for change within the structural planning framework. As most local streets and their utilities were located, financed, and constructed by the subdivider of land whose main aim was profit, ULI emphasized the advantages of reduced infrastructure: "There is a tendency in many municipalities to require excessive width for minor single family residential streets. This is reflected in a similar tendency to require excessive road pavements."[24]

ULI's desire to cut construction costs and to lessen the burden on developers was reflected in its recommendations for residential street construction, published in 1947:

- Right-of-way: maximum 50 feet (15.25 m)
- Pavement width: maximum 26 feet (8 m)
- Sidewalks: 4 feet (1.2 m) wide with regular curb, and 3 feet, 6 inches (1 m) with rolled curbs. "Sidewalks tend to encourage use of the street for play rather than off-street areas such as the rear yard or play ground. In general, the Council recommends a sidewalk on at least one side of the street."
- Curbs: "Rolled curbs are favored. They provide a pleasing unbroken street line, do not require expensive curb cuts, and are one of the most practical cost reducing items in street construction."
- Intersection radii: 15-foot (4.5 m) radius

- Planting strip: Recommended mainly for use with vertical curbs as a way to overcome the curb cuts and the gradient of the driveway. A minimum of 8 feet (2.4 m) on each side of the street was recommended for tree planting.[25]

ULI's publication of *Residential Streets* in 1974 and 1990 continued to advocate lower standards for local streets and also a renewed emphasis on accommodating other street uses than just vehicular access.[26, 27, 28]

An organization closely related to ULI was the National Association of Home Builders (NAHB), which also strongly opposed excessive standards. In its 1950s *Manual for Land Development* the organization asked: "Why is it that the widths of local residential roadways up to 36 and 40 feet are still advocated by some highway engineers and planning commissions?" That question is still being asked by many planners and designers today. The manual gave as the apparent reasons (1) misunderstanding of the relationship between street location, alignment width, and use; (2) adherence to the obsolete theory that every street should be designed to become a traffic street; (3) insistence on continuous alignment of minor streets; and (4) disregard of economic aspects such as the cost of constructing, maintaining, and repairing from 38 to 54 percent more roadway surface than is needed.[29]

Local planning agencies resisted the building industry's emphasis on reconsidering street standards. The threat of substandard street layouts along with the rise in vehicular ownership promoted a continuation of conservative design for subdivisions.

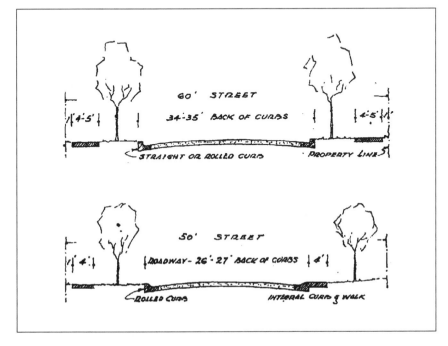

Representing the interests of land developers, ULI's 1947 recommended standards for residential streets reflected their desire to reduce construction costs through narrower roadways, rolled curbs, and integral curb and sidewalk designs. *(Urban Land Institute)*

ACCIDENTS AND GRIDS   The safety problems associated with through traffic in residential streets were first addressed by traffic engineers only in the mid-1950s, when the emphasis shifted to preventing through traffic by means of a hierarchical street network. Yet the cross sections of residential streets and their geometric configurations remained unchanged. One of the first engineering studies on street safety in residential subdivisions, conducted in Los Angeles between 1951 and 1956, examined the accident rates in developments with a grid pattern, as compared to the prevailing FHA limited-access and curvilinear patterns. The study included eighty-six residential subdivision tracts with a total developed area of 4,320 acres (1,728 ha), representing a population of 53,000 persons, 108 miles (173 km) of residential streets, and 660 intersections. The study results showed that accident rates were substantially higher for grid-pattern subdivisions: 77.7 accidents per year, as compared to 10.2 accidents per year for an equivalent area of limited-access subdivisions—a ratio of almost 8 to 1. Fifty percent of all intersections in the grid pattern had at least one accident during the five-year period. In contrast, only 8.8 percent of the intersections in the limited-access pattern had accidents during that period. This difference was particularly significant, since there were 65 percent more intersections in the limited-access tracts than in the grid tracts. Especially surprising was the number of T intersections with no accident record. Overall, T intersections were found to be fourteen times safer than four-leg intersections.[30] These performance-based findings enabled the traffic engineering profession to justify applying a discontinuous street pattern in residential subdivisions. Yet these studies should be interpreted cautiously, since the study seems to have several limitations including control of variables such as traffic volume and neighborhood density, topography, and pattern.

Expanding on the land use study and its findings, ITE produced a technical publication to establish engineering standards for the widely used discontinuous form of subdivision layout. In 1961 Harold Marks, the author of the Los Angeles study, presented a proposal for *Geometrics of Local and Collector Streets* to the 31st Annual Meeting of Traffic Engineers. The proposal called for a clear classification of streets: "One of the problems associated with the classification of streets is the lack of uniformity that presently prevails." It emphasized the need to adopt a residential system that would incorporate:

- Limited access to the perimeter highway
- Discontinuous local streets to discourage through traffic
- Design patterns with curvilinear alignment, cul-de-sacs, short street runs, and elbow turns
- A clear distinction between access streets and neighborhood collectors through section width
- Numerous three-leg T intersections
- Local street width with 40- to 60-foot (12.2–18.3 m) rights-of-way and 26- to 36-foot (8–11 m) pavements[31]

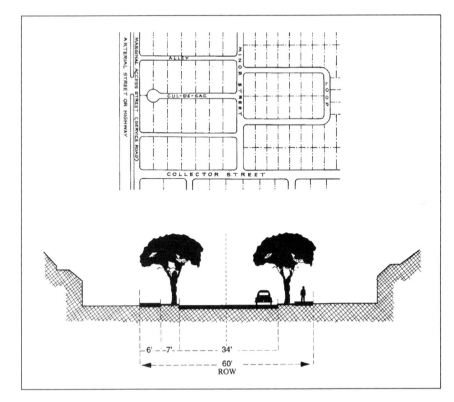

The Institute of Transportation Engineers residential street standards of 1965 and 1984 emphasize discontinuous patterns and a rather wide paved area. *(section: © Eran Ben-Joseph; plan: Institute of Transportation Engineers)*

In 1965, ITE's publication *Recommended Practice for Subdivision Streets* stated: "The primary objective of subdivision design is to provide maximum livability. This requires a safe and efficient access and circulation system, connecting homes, schools, playgrounds, shops and other subdivision activities for both pedestrians and vehicles."[32] Principles included:

- Circulation systems should be safe and efficient.
- Street systems should be designed in their entirety rather than piecemeal.
- Local street systems should be designed for a low volume of traffic and minimal through traffic.
- Local streets should be designed to discourage excessive speed through the use of curvilinear patterns and discontinuities.
- Pedestrian-vehicular conflict points should be minimized.
- A minimum amount of space should be devoted to streets.
- There should be minimal intersections with preference for T rather than four-leg intersections.
- Local streets should be related to topography.

The publication also proposed a set of standards for geometric configurations aimed mainly at efficient vehicular movement. They illustrate the

Simple engineering handbooks of street design standards have had a major impact on the American landscape. Presented as absolute and indisputable, they have become a rigid framework that allows little creativity and variation. They have shaped the overall pattern of neighborhoods and communities, as well as the quality and character of individual residential lots and streets.
(a: © William Garnett;
b: © Landslides, Alex S. MacLean;
c: © Michael Southworth)

conflict between flexible principles and the resulting set of rigid standards. ITE stated: "Although it is extremely important that sound standards be followed in the layout and design of neighborhoods and of neighborhood street systems, it is equally important that there be room for variety, experimentation and improvements in residential design." However, it prescribed these rigid standards:

- Right-of-way: minimum 60 feet (18.3 m)
- Pavement width: 32 to 34 feet (9.8–10.4 m)
- Curb: vertical curb with gutter, rolled curb not recommended
- Sidewalks: at both sides, minimum width 5 feet (1.5 m)

- Planting strip: 6 to 7 feet (1.8–2.1 m), sloping toward street
- Grade: minimum 4 percent, maximum 15 percent
- Cul-de-sac: maximum length 1,000 feet (305 m), with 50-foot (15.25 m) radius at end
- Parking lane: 8 feet (2.4 m)
- Driveway: minimum width of 10 feet (3 m) for one car, with 20-foot-wide (6 m) curb cut and 5-foot (1.5 m) flare at each side

When *Recommended Guidelines for Subdivision Streets* was published in 1984, the ITE standards and geometrical configurations remained practically unchanged from the 1965 version. In 1990 ITE's Technical Council Committee published another version, *Guidelines for Residential Subdivision Street Design*.[33] The main changes in this publication were a decrease of planting strip width to a minimum of 5 feet (1.5 m), and the extension of cul-de-sac length from 700 to 1,000 feet (213–305 m) with an increased end radius of 60 feet (18.3 m).

ITE standards have been widely used as the basis for subdivision regulation by local agencies and public works departments. It is remarkable how a simple handbook could have such impact on the way cities are built, and how little questioning and evaluation has been involved in their adoption. They established a professional framework and a reference source that could claim a scientific basis in empirical research. Despite the stated interest in variety and experimentation, the solution they provided was presented as absolute and indisputable, leaving little room for new design approaches. Within the engineering profession, there seems to have been little awareness or concern with the huge impacts these construction standards were having on the American landscape and the quality of neighborhoods.

Streets for Living

Rethinking Neighborhood Streets

If cities are to retain their populations, and if energy shortages force us back into concentrated cities, ways must be found in which city neighborhoods can be havens of rest after the day's work rather than precarious perches in a sea of noise, fumes, and dirt.

—Donald Appleyard, 1981

Today new developments continue to expand the edges of cities into new territory, but the deeply entrenched framework of standards still exerts its control over the form of the residential environment. How can we get out of this straitjacket? Are there approaches to changing the way new residential streets are built that would serve users better? Could existing patterns be improved upon? In this chapter we consider some promising possibilities.

In 1927 while designing Radburn, Clarence Stein called for a "revolution in planning." He challenged existing practices that were geared toward facilitating the automobile and proposed a "radical revision of relation of houses, roads, paths, gardens, parks, blocks, and local neighborhoods."[1] Stein's call for change has remained practically unanswered, and designers and planners are still searching for modifications to subdivision layouts.

The New Urbanism movement has offered one of the few alternatives to the suburban sprawl approach to development, the *neotraditional* community. Urban design has a long tradition of borrowing from the past, one that continues today as neotraditional designers look nostalgically back to the small American town as an alternative to conventional suburban development. These schemes echo the traditional patterns of walkable, mixed-use neighborhoods and suggest a return to some of the Garden City ideals of Unwin and Parker.

Compared with conventional suburbs, neotraditional developments, at least on the drawing board, are characterized by somewhat higher densities, mixed uses, provision of public transit, accommodation of the pedestrian and bicyclist, and a more interconnected pattern of streets. Two alternatives to the conventional low density auto-dependent suburban tract development have been proposed. One is the traditional neighborhood development (TND) or neotraditional development (NTD), which looks to the classic small town for its inspiration—it is walkable, has a clear civic structure, a mix of uses and housing types, and harmonious design of its buildings and spaces. The other alternative is the pedestrian pocket, sometimes referred to

LEARNING FROM TRADITIONAL STREET PATTERNS

as pedestrian-oriented development (POD) or transit-oriented development (TOD). It is similar to the neotraditional development in its concerns with walkability and convenient access, but there is less emphasis on controlling architectural form and emulating historical styles. According to one of its originators, Peter Calthorpe, it is "a mixed-use community within an average one-fourth mile walking distance of a transit stop and core commercial area. The design, configuration, and mix of uses emphasize a pedestrian-oriented environment and reinforce the use of public transportation."[2] Their designers assert that these approaches are less auto-dependent and will reduce travel distance and time, expand public transit use, and are more conducive to the formation of community sense than typical late twentieth century subdivisions.[3, 4]

Two neotraditional, transit-oriented developments are classic examples of their type: Kentlands in Gaithersburg, Maryland, a traditional neighborhood development designed by Andres Duany and Elizabeth Plater-Zyberk, and Laguna West, a pedestrian pocket or POD in greater Sacramento, California designed by Peter Calthorpe and Associates. We focus here primarily on their approaches to street design. For a baseline reference, it will be useful to compare these neotraditional developments with a traditional turn-of-the-century streetcar suburb, Elmwood in Berkeley, California. Several comparisons are also made with conventional suburbs of the late twentieth century.

Kentlands

Located on the historic 356-acre Kent family farm on the southwest edge of Gaithersburg, Maryland, Kentlands was designed in 1988 as a community of about 1600 dwelling units with a projected population of 5000. Surrounded by conventional suburban planned unit developments (PUDs) and auto-oriented commercial strips like other suburbs, it is not an independent community, but is dependent upon Gaithersburg and the larger metropolitan region for most services and jobs. One church, an elementary school, a day care center, and a community recreation center have been built, and a second church and library are proposed. One million square feet (90,000 sq m) of office space and 1.2 million square feet (91,800 sq m) of retail space were planned.

The gently rolling hills, mature trees, and pond of the old farm are significant features of the development. Organized into several distinct neighborhoods, the community avoids the monotony and lack of local identity of mass-produced suburbs. Neighborhoods include the Old Farm District that incorporates the restored original farm house, the Hill District, the Gatehouse District, the Lake District, and Midtown/Downtown, a local commercial center adjacent to the shopping mall. A major structural statement is the divided boulevard connecting the west entry circle at the school site with the semicircular recreation center site. Landmark structures terminate vistas at several points. A relatively fine and varied grain, mix of housing types, and coherent pattern has been achieved in the residential areas.

Streets of the neotraditional development of Kentlands are very different from typical late twentieth century suburbs. They are relatively narrow, and are bordered by sidewalks and planting strips with trees. The traditional architectural styles and street details create an instant "historic" image.
(© Michael Southworth)

The sense of Kentlands is markedly different from conventional suburban development, with strong architectural references to the past that blend Federal, Classical Revival, and other styles. The feeling of the development recalls older, intimately scaled towns in the Maryland/Virginia vernacular with white picket fences, porches, and picturesque alleyways and carriage house courts. An instant "historic" image has been created for the place, although it is a rather pleasant image that blends with the authentic history

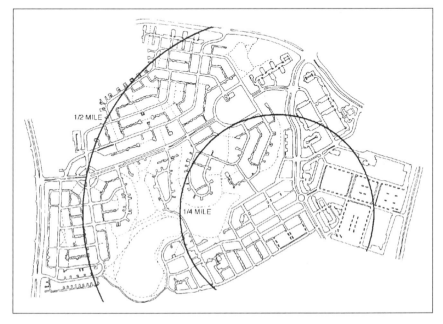

In Kentlands the street grid is organized into several neighborhoods, each with its own character. The pedestrian network is fine-grained and explorable. Street patterns are generally well-interconnected, offering several different ways to move through the area. Garages are placed behind the houses and are accessed via alleys. (© Michael Southworth)

of the old farm buildings. An enormously important ingredient of its character is the landscape that retains many mature trees and topographic features. Grading and siting of buildings have been unusually sensitive to the natural setting. Provision of alleys for garage access has a major impact on street character by eliminating garage doors and driveways from streets. Moreover, the back lanes and carriage house courts are often charming and explorable places.

Laguna West

Set on a flat, treeless former rice paddy, the 1,018-acre (407 ha) site of Laguna West is almost three times the size of Kentlands. Begun in 1990, it is projected to have about twice as many residents: 3,300 dwelling units and a population of 8,000 to 10,000. Besides residential areas, there is to be a community center with civic, retail, and office space, as well as a church, day care center, and one elementary school. Light industrial space is adjacent to the center and includes an operating Apple Computer plant. Located about 12 miles (19 km) south of downtown Sacramento, but outside the city limits, recent tract developments of conventional design surround Laguna West but are weakly interconnected. Like Kentlands, it will function as part of the larger metropolitan region for jobs and services. It is within a half-hour commuting distance to both downtown Sacramento and Stockton.

The most striking design features of Laguna West are the formal axial layout and lagoons that at first glance might suggest Versailles superimposed on Irvine. According to the designers, the radial scheme is intended to compensate for the flat uninteresting site by creating a strong focus and a grand scale. Three axes converge on a community center, which is to contain pedestrian-

One innovation in some of the streets of Laguna West is the placement of trees in wells within the paved area. The intent is to define the parking area and, ultimately, to create the sense of a narrower street. *(© Eran Ben-Joseph)*

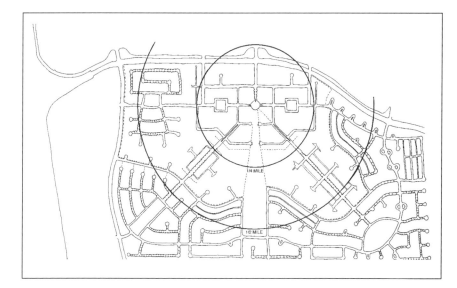

accessible retail and office space. Two of these axes are vehicular streets over one-half mile long that lead from the community center into neighborhoods; the center axis is a greenway that leads to a park, elementary school, and day care center. Major shallow artificial lakes define the southern edge of the community center and intersect the axes, ostensibly purifying runoff by natural means before entering the adjacent wetland. Compared with Kentlands the built form pattern is more coarse and repetitive, and lacks the mixing of housing types and sizes at the scale of individual blocks. It also lacks a sense of clearly differentiated neighborhoods which does so much to make Kentlands an interesting place to live.

Laguna West, in contrast to Kentlands, has the sense of a late twentieth century suburb with rows of single family homes lined up along barren curving streets. There are subtle differences, however. There is a much stronger sense of "streetscape" than in most suburbs since many houses have front porches and yards, and garages are set to the side or back, avoiding the "garagescape" street image. In contrast to Kentlands, there is much less apparent architectural control and historicism. Presumably this was intentional in order to attract Sacramento home buyers.

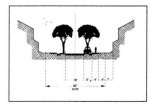

Laguna West Street section.
(© Eran Ben-Joseph)

Elmwood: A Traditional Streetcar Suburb

Traditional developments offer a useful comparison with neotraditional models such as Kentlands and Laguna West. Although they were developed in different economic, social, and technological frameworks and have had decades to mature, much can be learned about the scale and arrangement of streets in relation to activities, built form, and public spaces. Begun early in the twentieth century, the Elmwood district of Berkeley is much like streetcar suburbs of the same era found in other parts of the country. Originally an

In Elmwood, each street is unique. Sidewalks and planting strips line the relatively narrow streets. Homes were built individually on a lot-by-lot basis, so there is much more variety than in suburbs of today. Front porches provide a transitional space to the street. (© Michael Southworth)

The street pattern of Elmwood, a streetcar suburb dating from the early 1900s, is a rectilinear grid, with blocks that vary in size and shape. There are no formal design features. "Berkeley Barriers" have been installed to convert the interconnected grid to a limited access pattern for motorists. (© Michael Southworth)

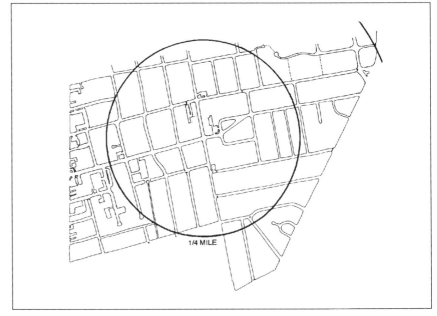

1/4 MILE

area of large estates, these were subdivided into several tracts in the housing boom following the 1906 San Francisco earthquake. Like most other streetcar suburbs, Elmwood began as a true suburb, set in open land away from the central city, but after nearly a century of urban infill and expansion, it has become an integral part of the San Francisco East Bay metropolis. Today it is a pleasant walkable neighborhood of what appear to be mainly single-family homes, but some of these have been adapted for apartments or duplexes.

In pattern the Elmwood district is a modified rectilinear grid made up of blocks of varied sizes; the grain of the built form is fine and varied. Unlike the neotraditional models, it has no obvious formal design elements. In an area of about 225 acres (90 ha), less than two-thirds the size of Kentlands, there are approximately 2,300 dwelling units including about 1,100 single-family residences housing a total population of approximately 5,000.

Elmwood, in contrast to both Kentlands and Laguna West, seems to have grown more incrementally, creating a homey, comfortable feeling. Built before the era of mega-developers, homes were constructed individually on a lot-by-lot basis by varied builders and architects, and they are of many styles, from Craftsman shingle, to Classical Revival or Mediterranean. The hand of a single designer or planner is not felt. Houses have front porches that provide a transitional space from the street, and garages are typically small and situated near the rear corner of the lot. Sidewalks with planting strips line the relatively narrow streets. Each street is unique and mature trees contribute much visual interest.

Neotraditional Street Design and Pattern

Neotraditional advocates argue that standard suburban residential streets limit access capacity by their discontinuous pattern. By eliminating dead-ends and designing most streets to be interconnected, neotraditional design provides multiple-route choices for trips. In concept, therefore, overall network capacity is increased, traffic is dispersed, and congestion is reduced. However, the rhetoric sometimes exceeds reality.

In contrast to typical suburban street design, neotraditional design calls for narrower streets. The basic street is composed of two lanes, one for each direction, and space for parking on at least one side. The resulting minimum width may be as narrow as 28 to 30 feet (8.5–9.2 m). By encouraging on-street parking, neotraditional proponents argue that a row of parked vehicles enhances pedestrian activity by creating a buffer between pedestrians and moving traffic. Traffic engineers, on the other hand, are often overly concerned about on-street parking, in particular that it will increase "dart-out" accidents, where pedestrians—especially children—run from between parked vehicles into the traffic lane. Experience suggests that such concerns can be easily mitigated through the control of speed and traffic volumes. Furthermore, changes to the street physical design can control driver behavior and alleviate potential conflicts.

In both Kentlands and Laguna West, as well as Elmwood, local streets are somewhat narrower than in conventional developments and are provided with sidewalks and street trees that are maintained by the community; both features are unusual in suburban developments today. Street patterns are more interconnected with less use of loops and cul-de-sacs, particularly in Kentlands. Both neotraditional developments also incorporate formal design elements rarely found in conventional suburbs: axial streets in Laguna West and a divided boulevard connecting two formal civic spaces in Kentlands.

In Kentlands, streets are relatively narrow: within the 50-foot (15.25 m) right-of-way, the 36-foot (11 m) pavement consists of two 10-foot (3 m) driving lanes and two 8-foot (2.45 m) parking lanes. They are provided with 4- to 5-foot (1.2–1.5 m) sidewalks and a planting strip throughout. Alleys are 26 feet (8 m) wide with a 12-foot (3.6 m) paved lane and 7-foot (2 m) grass strips on each side. Street trees are maintained by the city and line both sides of wider streets, but only one side of narrower streets. There are numerous straight, parallel streets and right-angle intersections, as well as alleys. However, the street layouts of each district vary and, when combined with alleys and carriage house courts, a very explorable network is created. Streets are organized largely in modified, warped grid patterns—not a checkerboard—with some use of cul-de-sacs in the alleys and loops near the lake. Some neighborhoods have less interconnectedness than others; for example, vehicular connections between the Midtown/Downtown district and other districts is tenuous because of the location of the wetland. Pedestrian and bicycle networks are quite intricate and well connected, with every district having numerous alternate pathways. Many of these pathways parallel the streets and alleys. Most of the pedestrian routes offer visual interest, with small-scale detail and variety, as well as changing vistas and focal points. The pathways would seem to work well for children playing and visiting friends and for adult recreation, but it is unlikely they would satisfy routine functional needs except for those who live near the shopping center, recreation center, or school.

In Laguna West, a major design statement is made with the three axial boulevards radiating from the center, but much of the street network on which these are overlaid is not strikingly different from that of other suburbs where few streets are straight and cul-de-sacs are plentiful. Street patterns within the residential areas are modified, warped grid patterns with a number of cul-de-sacs. Unlike some suburbs, there are sidewalks and some areas have a gravel jogging trail. Given its flat, barren terrain, and unfinished state, it is not an interesting place to walk. Major streets are standard width to accommodate fire trucks, but local streets are narrower—30 feet (9.2 m). One major difference compared with conventional suburbs is the placement of trees in wells that project into the street space and break up the parking strip on the axial streets and in some neighborhood locations. When the trees mature they will create the sense of a narrower street, but presently some residents complain that the wells are difficult to see and are hazardous, particularly when they lack trees.

The street pattern of Elmwood, a modified rectilinear grid with blocks of varying sizes, has no formal design features, although certain streets have thematic street trees. Four-way intersections predominate, but there are a few T intersections, five cul-de-sacs, and one loop. Mature trees shade the narrow streets (30 to 34 feet [9.2–10.4 m] wide), which have parking, as well as sidewalks with narrow planting strips along both sides. To create quieter and safer streets "Berkeley Barriers," discussed later, were installed midstreet to convert the interconnected grid pattern into one primarily of loops and cul-de-sacs for the motorist. These have, in effect, added 15 cul-de-sacs to the street pattern. However, it is important to note that grid continuity is maintained for the pedestrian and bicyclist, a quality lacking in most suburban cul-de-sac developments.

Comparing Street Patterns

Street patterns contribute significantly to the quality and character of a community. The total amount of land devoted to streets relates directly to infrastructure costs. The number of blocks, intersections, access points, and loops or cul-de-sacs per unit area affect the number of route options and ease of moving about. Comparing the street patterns illustrates that Elmwood is clearly the most rectilinear of the developments. It also has the least amount of street within the unit analyzed—18,000 feet (5,500 m)—despite its high level of interconnectedness; Kentlands has 24,000 feet (7,300 m) and Laguna West has 19,000 feet (5,800 m). Elmwood and Kentlands have about the same number of blocks, 23 and 24 blocks per unit area, but Laguna West has only 16. Elmwood and Laguna West have the same number of intersections, 20 per unit area. However, Kentlands has 41 blocks per unit area, more than twice as many because of the large number of alleys. These create more route choices and thus a more explorable fine-grained network. In terms of access into the study areas from outside, Kentlands has 22 points of entry to the study area, while Elmwood has 16, and Laguna West has only 14. However, when the entire development is examined compared with Elmwood, both Kentlands and Laguna West are weakly connected with the surrounding urban context. In this sense they are no different than other suburban planned unit developments. Finally, when traditional and neotraditional patterns are analyzed in terms of loops and cul-de-sacs—the essence of discontinuous suburban street forms—Elmwood has only 1 (8 including the traffic barriers); however, Laguna West with 15 loops and cul-de-sacs in the study area and Kentlands with 10 are far more suburban than Elmwood.

Comparing these patterns with suburban patterns of the 1960s through the 1980s, the neotraditional patterns generally have more lineal feet of street, more blocks, more intersections, and more access points than conventional suburbs, making them more costly to build and maintain. They have fewer loops and cul-de-sacs than the most recent suburban patterns ("lollipops on a stick"), but more than earlier suburban patterns such as the "warped parallel" pattern of the 1960s and the "loops and lollipops" pattern of the 1970s and 1980s. Thus, neotraditional developments have made some gains in providing route choice and convenience.

Another comparison between the recently built neotraditional neighborhood of Belmont, Virginia and a typical development planned on the same site highlights these arguments. Overall, the neotraditional development has 50 percent more street miles than the typical subdivision design. There are

Comparative Analysis of Traditional and Neotraditional Street Patterns. Elmwood is clearly the most rectilinear pattern and has the least amount of street length. Laguna West is more like other suburbs in terms of number of blocks, access to the larger context, and number of loops and cul-de-sacs. Squares are 2,000 feet on each side and contain approximately 100 acres. (© Michael Southworth)

	ELMWOOD (1905)	KENTLANDS (1989)	LAGUNA WEST (1990s)
Street Patterns			
Intersections			
Lineal Feet of Streets	18,000	24,000 (alleys 7, 000)	19,000
Number of Blocks	23	24 (w.o. alleys 14)	16
Number of Intersections	20	41 (with alleys)	20
Number of Access Points	17	22	14
Number of Loops & Cul-de-sacs	1	10	15

nearly 50 percent more lane miles of street capacity, and nearly a third more street intersections, as well as 73 percent more acres of right-of-way. This additional acreage and greater street mileage resulted in higher infrastructure costs that were ultimately passed on to the home buyers.[5]

The rise of neotraditional design concepts has prompted a few transportation studies by the traffic engineering profession. As none of the neotraditional communities are fully operational, computer modeling has been used to examine the assertion that a neotraditional street network will reduce travel distance and time and lessen automobile dependency. Computer modeling suggests that a neotraditional street network will function more efficiently than a conventional suburban network by increasing route choice. The employment of multiple routes and intersections will provide more connections and avoid loading traffic on one street in particular. Although such a street system has a potential for easing congestion on main streets, it will also add through traffic on residential streets.[6,7] The increase of

	Gridiron (c. 1900)	Fragmented Parallel (c. 1950)	Warped Parallel (c. 1960)	Loops and Lollipops (c. 1970)	Lollipops on a Stick (c. 1980)
Street Patterns					
Intersections					
Lineal Feet of Streets	20,800	19,000	16,500	15,300	15,600
# of Blocks	28	19	14	12	8
# of Intersections	26	22	14	12	8
# of Access Points	19	10	7	6	4
# of Loops & Cul-de-Sacs	0	1	2	8	24

Comparative Analysis of Suburban Street Patterns. Compared with suburban patterns of the 1960s through 1980s, neotraditional patterns generally have more total street length, more blocks, more intersections, and more access points. This means they provide more route choice and convenience. (© Michael Southworth and Peter Owens)

automobile accessibility on minor residential streets raises issues of cut-through traffic and excessive speed through residential areas and might prove to be an obstacle to increasing pedestrianization and social interaction in neighborhoods.

Pedestrian Access

Pedestrian networks are, of course, an integral part of street design. In the neotraditional developments pedestrian access is promoted through sidewalks, some exclusive pedestrian and bicycle ways, and through an attempt to create a path network that interconnects destinations such as parks, schools, civic facilities, and shops and services. Unlike most suburbs, both Kentlands and Laguna West try to integrate retail and office space by inserting a pedestrian-oriented shopping/office center into the development. The attempt cannot be said to be entirely successful to date.

Several researchers have found that the distance Americans will walk for typical daily trips is quite limited, varying from 400 feet (120 m) to about 1/4 mile (400 m). Untermann found that 70 percent of Americans will walk 500 feet (150 m) for daily errands and that 40 percent will walk 1/5 mile (320 m); only 10 percent will walk 1/2 mile (800 m).[8] Similarly, Barber found that the distance people walked for typical trips varied between 400 and 1,200 feet (120–370 m).[9] If these findings also apply to residents of neotraditional developments, the distances to many of the retail and service centers, especially in Laguna West, are too great to expect most residents to walk to them on a regular basis. The land use patterns do not help, since commercial areas are situated on the periphery rather than in the center of both developments. Thus, for most residents these communities are likely to remain auto-oriented like other suburbs. The difference is that there is a network of pedestrian routes that can be used for recreation by children and adults. Provision of fine-grained and well-connected pedestrian routes that offer visual interest help make walking and bicycling enjoyable. According to informal reports, people from surrounding areas often drive to Kentlands for the sole purpose of taking walks because it is more interesting and walkable than most other suburbs. While the site does accommodate retail and commercial uses, residential connections to them are still somewhat auto-dependent. Most homes are a 5- to 10-minute walk from the shopping center (1/4 to 1/2 mile [400–800 m]). Although the designers fought for a more intimate connection between the shopping center and residential areas, the demands of automobile-oriented marketing have resulted in a shopping mall segregated on the opposite side of a major arterial street. In Laguna West the center has not yet materialized—except for the community recreation building, the commercial sites are unbuilt. About half of the residences will be more than a 10-minute walk (1/2 mile [800 m]) from the community center.

Although Elmwood has no exclusive pedestrian or bicycle routes, the neighborhood works quite well for both, allowing interconnection and through-movement, while the barriers restrict and slow vehicular traffic. The neighborhood, which admittedly has had nearly a century to mature, has a lively and quite successful local commercial center. Unlike the neotraditional developments, the commercial district is centrally located on College Avenue and has numerous basic services, restaurants, and specialty shops. In time, both neotraditional developments might also support successful centers, but because of the land use patterns and density, they can never be as convenient as Elmwood.

How suitable are these developments for those most dependent upon pedestrian access: children, teenagers, and elderly? The denser distribution and interconnection of a wider variety of spaces and destinations in Kentlands provides greater access and activity opportunities than Laguna West. Alleys provide a different kind of space, perhaps a more interesting place for teenagers and children to "hang out." Alleys also provide more visual access to backyards, the suburban hideaways. Although alleys probably reduce privacy, they may promote more casual neighboring and spontaneity. Laguna West has less variety of street spaces for children's play and access to regional activity centers is currently difficult; for teenagers, it would probably seem a boring place to live much like any suburb. However, the lake areas could potentially be a special attraction for them, but there is only one park that fronts on the lake. Provision of sidewalks serves needs of children and elderly in both developments by making neighborhoods more explorable on foot, as well as on bicycle and skateboard for children. Except for its lack of local parks, Elmwood would seem to serve the needs of youth and elderly quite well, since it is walkable, has generally safe streets, and excellent access to the College Avenue shopping district. In addition, it has good access by transit to the larger city and region.

In conclusion, both neotraditional examples discussed here have a stronger sense of public structure than conventional suburbs. They also offer more interesting and cohesive streetscape, and Kentlands stands out in its sensitivity to the landscape and creation of interesting streets and pedestrian ways. However, neither of the developments achieves the ease of access to retail and office uses, mix of housing types, pedestrian access to daily needs, and overall connectedness found in many small towns or early twentieth-century streetcar suburbs which the neotraditional models emulate. At minimum, they represent modest improvements over most conventional suburban planned unit developments.

One of the most intriguing design innovations of the last twenty years has been the shared street or integration concept for residential streets. That the street is properly a physical and social part of the living environment, and is used simultaneously for vehicular movement, social contacts, and civic activities, has long been argued by many authors including Kevin Lynch, Donald Appleyard, Jane Jacobs, J. B. Jackson, and William Whyte. However, these characteristics of traditional European and American streets, though still found in many neighborhoods of American inner cities, have long disappeared from contemporary American suburbs. Yet in suburbs of European and other foreign cities a major shift in residential street design has occurred. In countries such as The Netherlands, Germany, England, Australia, Japan, and Israel, the integration of traffic and residential activity in the same space is a concept that has stimulated new design configurations that increase social interaction and safety on the street and promote pedestrian movement.[10–15]

The underlying concept of the shared street system is one of integration, with an emphasis on the community and the residential user. Pedestrians, children at play, bicyclists, parked cars, and moving cars all share the same street space. Even though it seems these uses conflict with each other, the physical design is such that drivers are placed in an inferior position. Such conditions are actually much safer for the pedestrian than in common residential street layouts. By redesigning the physical aspects of the street, the social and physical public domain of the pedestrian is reclaimed. Since this "emancipation" of the pedestrian environment is done with full integration of vehicular traffic, it is not an anticar policy.

The shared street concept gained popularity in Europe and has been applied in several countries, most notably in The Netherlands where it was first developed and executed. Its philosophical roots can be found in a 1963 report published in England by Colin Buchanan and the *Traffic in Towns* team.[16] In 1959 the Ministry of Transportation commissioned Buchanan to investigate the issue of improving urban transport.[17] This was to be done "both in terms of reducing congestion and to come to terms with the car." Buchanan, a road engineer as well as an architect, brought to the team an innovative point of view. He was able to see the conflict between providing for

THE SHARED STREET CONCEPT

In the shared street or *woonerf*, pedestrians and vehicles share the same space, which is designed to slow traffic and to support play and social uses. Since motorists sense they are intruding into a pedestrian zone, they drive more cautiously and accident rates decline.
(© *Eran Ben-Joseph*)

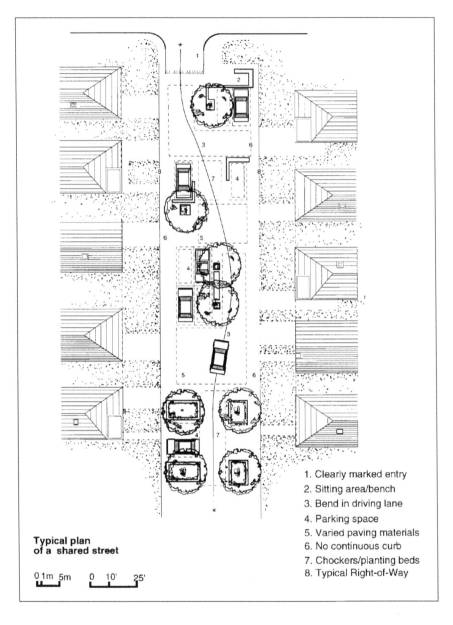

1. Clearly marked entry
2. Sitting area/bench
3. Bend in driving lane
4. Parking space
5. Varied paving materials
6. No continuous curb
7. Chockers/planting beds
8. Typical Right-of-Way

**Typical plan
of a shared street**

0 1m 5m   0   10'   25'

easy traffic flow and the destruction of the residential and architectural fabric of the street. In the context of the prevailing philosophy of the late 1950s and early 1960s this was a unique, if not revolutionary, approach. The team came up with a technique for evaluating and restructuring the urban traffic system by creating specific zones, which they called *environmental areas* or *urban rooms*. These were to be of a different character from typical streets, with traffic levels that would vary according to their functions. Streets would not only be evaluated in terms of their capacity to carry traffic, but also environmental quality as measured by noise, pollution, social activity, pedestrianization, and visual aesthetics. This criterion of environmental capacity would then be used in setting standards and limitations.[18] Thus, certain environmental areas would segregate traffic and pedestrians completely, while others would allow pedestrians and vehicles to mix safely in the street. The public domain would be reclaimed for pedestrians by redesigning the physical aspects of the street.

In the beginning the concepts of "traffic integration" and "traffic calming" in the environmental capacity zones were not well received by the British policymakers, since they seemed to run counter to the major governmental policies of promoting economic development through road construction and railway improvements. However, the report surfaced again in the late 1970s and provided its major impact when the British Government combined two departments, the Ministry of Transport and the Ministry of Housing and Local Government, into the new Department of the Environment.[19] This was the first attempt to address both land use issues and transportation planning as a single entity, yet physical changes were slow to appear.

Interestingly, the *Traffic in Towns* report had much more impact in continental Europe. German and Dutch planners enthusiastically adopted the ideas and many still refer to Buchanan as the "father of traffic calming." In The Netherlands, Buchanan's theoretical concepts inspired Niek De Boer, professor of urban planning at Delft University of Technology and the University of Emmen. Trying to overcome the contradiction between streets as places for children's play, as well as car use, he saw in Buchanan's concept of coexistence a possible solution. He designed streets so that motorists

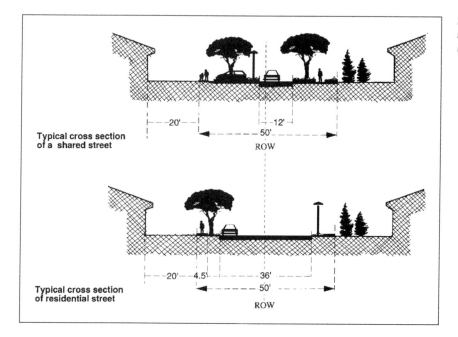

Typical cross section of a shared street

20' · 12' · 50' · ROW

Typical cross section of residential street

20' · 4.5' · 36' · 50' · ROW

Shared Street Sections: shared street and typical street.
(© Eran Ben-Joseph)

Shared streets have been successful in many countries, including the Netherlands (a), Israel (b), and Tokyo (c). *(a: © Tim Pharoah; b: © Eran Ben-Joseph; c: The Wheel Extended)*

would feel as if they were driving in a "garden" setting, forcing drivers to consider other road users. De Boer renamed the street a *woonerf*, or "residential yard." At the same time, in 1969 the Municipality of Delft, which was considering redesigning and upgrading road surfaces in inner-city locations, decided to implement De Boer's ideas in some of the lower-income neighborhoods where more child play areas were urgently needed, but which lacked play sites. With resident participation, the design integrated sidewalks and roadways into one surface, creating the impression of a yard. Trees, benches, and small front gardens further enhanced the space.[20, 21]

The Delft experience was a success and the *woonerf* concept spread throughout The Netherlands in the form of guidelines and regulations. The first set of minimum design standards and traffic regulations for the *woonerf*

was adopted and legalized by the Dutch government in 1976. A brief excerpt from the *Traffic Regulations for the Woonerf*,[22] translated from Dutch, illustrates their innovative and rigorous nature:

- **Article 88a RVV**
  Pedestrians may use the full width of the highway within an area defined as a "*Woonerf*"; playing on the roadway is also permitted.

- **Article 88b RVV**
  Drivers within a "*Woonerf*" may not drive faster than at a walking pace. They must make allowance for the possible presence of pedestrians, including children at play, unmarked objects and irregularities in the road surface, and the alignment of the roadway.

113

These regulations were the basis of the guidelines for shared streets adopted shortly thereafter in many other countries: in Germany in 1976, in England, Sweden, and Denmark in 1977, in France and Japan in 1979, in Israel in 1981, and in Switzerland in 1982. By 1990 over 3,500 shared streets had been constructed in The Netherlands and Germany, more than 300 in Japan, and 600 in Israel. In some new residential areas the concept was so popular that it became the major type of street. In each country it is called by a different name: *wohnstraßen*, or *living street*, in Germany; *shared street* or *mixed court* in England; *community doro*, or *community street*, in Japan; and *rehov meshulav*, or *integrated street*, in Israel. Today, *unified street system* is a global term that encompasses the basic ideas represented by the original *woonerf*.[23–30]

Design Characteristics of Shared Streets

Shared streets integrate pedestrian activity and vehicular movement on one shared surface. In this approach the street has first and foremost the functions of a residence, a playground, and a meeting area. It has the additional functions of carrying access traffic and providing parking spaces, but is not designed for intentional through traffic. The unified street system is fully adaptable to any residential street setting and to various physical shapes. Looking at the evolution of the form since its inception, several design characteristics are typical:

- It is a residential, public space.
- Through traffic is discouraged.
- Paved space is shared by pedestrians and cars, with pedestrians having priority over the entire street. Walking and playing are allowed everywhere.
- It can be a single street, a square (or other form), or a combination of connected spaces.
- Its entrances are clearly marked.
- There are no conventional, straight stretches of pavement with raised curbs, and the pavement (carriageway) and sidewalk (footway) are not rigidly demarcated.
- Car speed and movement are restricted by physical barriers and deviations, bends, and undulations.
- Residents have automobile access to their dwelling fronts.
- The area has extensive landscaping and street furnishings.

Typically the entire right-of-way is paved in the same way, often with a special paving texture such as brick or stone. Elimination of curb and grade changes creates a continuous surface and enhances the sense of continuous space. Even when a curb is needed for drainage purposes, the same paving material usually covers the entire space. Such features have a powerful effect on drivers. Without the familiar two-curb lines and an asphalt roadway, drivers tend to slow down. A "restrictive" approach, on the other hand, can use any number of devices to intimidate drivers so that they are inclined to slow down: tight curves, narrow pavements, natural obstacles such as trees or rocks, visual cues such as pavement color, and rough pavements. Directional changes and the placement of planting beds provide further driver inhibition. Drivers must negotiate and pass through narrow sections of roadway which are just over 11 feet (3.3 m) wide, allowing the passage of one car at a time in a two-way traffic situation (the width might vary to allow clear passage for local service vehicles). The traveled route shifts from side to side every 125 feet (40 m), discouraging speed buildup. Planting beds are laid out in a manner that does not obstruct the passing of large emergency vehicles; they are usually low—12 inches (30 cm) high—and are made from durable materials. Their height and material allow large vehicles, such as a hook-and-ladder firetruck, to drive over them in case of an emergency; they do not hinder the opening of car doors and can provide informal seating.

Parking design follows a variety of patterns. In some configurations spaces are clustered together in groups of no more than six spaces and are at a right angle to traffic. This layout demands more attention from the driver and can be better used by children when the spaces are empty. Other patterns provide parking spaces near dwelling entrances. Such schemes satisfy residents' desires to park as close as possible to their homes. Parking is not a hindrance to the aesthetic quality of the street. In many designs parking spaces are not clearly marked. The early practices of marking parking areas with signs and paving have been replaced by physical elements; planting beds, street furniture, and trees define the spaces where parked cars can fit. While visually the street is perceived as one coherent unit, the underlying physical structure controls driver conduct in through movements and parking.

Although most of these physical characteristics apply to a linear street layout, the unified street principles can be applied to any configuration. In 1974 the concept of shared streets was introduced in Britain for new developments. By allowing clusters of houses to be accessed by pedestrians and drivers through a shared undemarcated surface, designers were able to develop new urban forms. With favorable reaction from residents, the British Department of the Environment and the Department of Transportation published a set of guidelines for shared surface design in 1977.[31] Recently, new town developments in Japan and Israel have incorporated the unified street concept as a basic design layout, as well. In these developments most residential streets are shared spaces branching off a main collector. Both pedestrians and drivers reach the clusters of houses across a shared undemarcated surface. This arrangement has freed designers to develop new spatial patterns, unconstrained by the regularity of linear streets.

The Social Benefits

Shared streets establish a social milieu and make the street a mixed-use public domain as it was prior to mass ownership of the automobile. More than transportation channels, streets are places suited for pedestrian interaction, where people choose to pause and socialize. They are especially supportive of children's activities, providing more play options and social contact within a safe home-base territory. Residents of shared streets tend to view the street as an extension of their personal space and often maintain and landscape the planting beds near their homes. Research indicates that as people spend more time on the street, the chances for social interaction also increase. This is particularly true for children's play. A study of two *woonerven* in Hanover, Germany before and after conversion revealed that street redesign led to a 20 percent increase in play activity, as well as a greater variety of activities. Children stayed longer, and without adult supervision, and play became more complex. Games requiring more space and the use of bicycles and toy vehicles also increased. Most notable was the shift in play location: from narrow street sidewalks to the *woonerf*'s entire width, including the former traffic lane.[32]

Similar studies in Japan report that 90 percent of those surveyed said the shared street was for people's use rather than for automobile use; 67 percent said that their children played in the street and that it was considered a safe place to play. People expressed great satisfaction with a street space that could be used for more than one purpose, and with the fact that children could play throughout, not just in the play lots or sidewalks. A majority of the residents (66 percent) felt that the shared street encouraged social interaction and conversation between neighbors.[33]

A study of shared streets in Germany before and after conversion revealed that shared streets attracted more play activity, and more complex activity, without adult supervision, than regular streets before conversion.
(© Eubank)

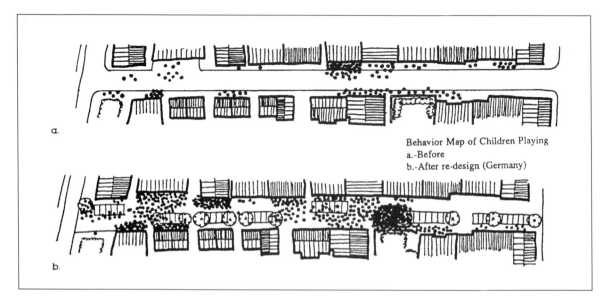

Behavior Map of Children Playing
a.-Before
b.-After re-design (Germany)

a.

b.

Shared streets make the street space a mixed-use public domain for a variety of activities like playing, talking, relaxing, watching, or gardening. *(© Eran Ben-Joseph)*

Surveys in Israel also showed that shared streets foster encounters and communication between neighbors. Most residents preferred a dead-end street (cul-de-sac) to a through one-way street, indicating that a dead-end street improved the environment and safety of their neighborhood. The majority of the children (81 percent) played in the street every day, using it as their main play zone. Between 88 and 100 percent of the residents said they were willing to maintain the public planting beds within the streets, and almost 50 percent said they were actually doing so.[34, 35]

A nationwide study in The Netherlands indicates that residents' attitudes toward shared streets are strongly influenced by the level of satisfaction with the design and social performance of the public spaces, rather than by the functioning of the traffic system.[36, 37] Moreover, residents are willing to accept restraints on traffic and driving in order to improve their social and residential environment. The surveys found that mothers, as well as children, consider the shared street safer than an ordinary street. It is also clear that the amount of knowledge one has about shared streets directly corresponds with attitudes toward them. Thus, opposition to implementation is mainly correlated with general lack of knowledge about the shared street concept.

Safety

Even though it might seem that vehicular traffic and pedestrians would be in conflict, the physical design of shared streets actually subordinates the traffic, a situation that is much safer for the pedestrian than the usual street layout. In terms of safety, studies in Germany, Denmark, Japan, and Israel show that there are over 20 percent fewer accidents in shared streets and over 50 percent fewer severe accidents compared with standard residential streets. The groups that benefit the most are pedestrians, children, and cyclists.[38, 39] The most prevalent traffic accidents on standard residential streets are child-related accidents. According to a study in England, half of all road accidents with children under five occur within 100 meters of their homes. The same survey showed that very few such accidents occur on streets with restrictive devices and shared surfaces or cul-de-sac design.[40] The suggestion often encountered, that safety improvements in one area increase the accidents in neighboring areas, was not proven. Interestingly, the safety results in Europe and in Asia appear to be similar.[41–49]

Another promising finding showed a reduction of vehicle trips of up to 14 percent.[50] The performance of pavement types was studied in Japan; fewer traffic accidents and safer driving were found when interlocking pavers were used. The use of different colors and the vibrations of the blocks make drivers slow down, in addition to reducing the distance required for a complete stop when compared with asphalt paving.[51]

These results are contrary to the logic of most road engineering. What is the explanation? The shared street layout establishes a pedestrian orientation by giving pedestrians primary rights; the driver is the intruder and is forced to realize he/she is entering a zone where the pedestrian has preeminent privileges. The motorist then recognizes the probability of sudden conflicts and exercises particular caution. This combination of an alerted driver and low vehicle speed substantially reduce the likelihood of a serious accident; the maximum speed in a shared street was recorded at 13.5 mph (21.8 kph).[52]

Prospects for Shared Streets in Suburbia

The shared street concept and its design implementation deviate from the typical standardization of street design. Shared streets require a more receptive and flexible design approval procedure that does not adhere to prescriptive solutions. Its success lies in creating a workable compromise between conflicting interests, both within the physical domain of the street and within the planning and engineering professions. It provides an example of a street design that follows what Thomas Adams in 1934 called "guidance rather than law."[53]

Unfortunately, the *woonerf* concept has remained little more than a novelty in North America. Although the idea was discussed in Donald Appleyard's 1981 book *Livable Streets*, and in ITE's 1989 publication *Residential Street Design and Traffic Control*,[54] it has not gained the acceptance of legislative and planning agencies. Public agencies have seen no need to initiate such a concept and developers have preferred the "sure approved plan" over any new concept that might entangle their project in a bureaucratic web. There are other possible reasons for resistance, as well. Individual property rights and sense of privacy are very strong in America, and there is not as strong a tradition of collective ownership as in Europe. There are also more and larger automobiles per household, which take up more space for storage and movement. In addition, municipalities and developers are concerned about liability in a situation that does not conform to established standards and where rights are not clearly defined. Engineering and public works departments, which have guided the development and management of residential streets, have often hesitated to adopt traffic management schemes for fear of lawsuits by drivers, passengers, or pedestrians. The new trend of neotraditional design, however, by challenging established standards and regulations, has stirred an important debate about the future of residential development that has extended to the transportation and civil engineering professions.

There is no doubt that shared streets would be suitable for certain residential street layouts in the United States. This very adaptable concept has been synthesized and reshaped in many countries to fit local regulations and needs. Several situations might be ideal for the shared street in the American context. Multifamily housing developments, with large numbers of children and only local traffic, could expand usable open space, as well as improve appearance of automobile access and storage areas using the shared street concept. Another obvious application would be suburban cul-de-sacs and loops, which already have limited traffic and are often used for play purposes. Conversion to a *woonerf* type of space with appropriate paving and planting would be an enormous improvement in the suburban landscape. Medium-density urban residential streets, too, might be suitable candidates for redesign. The shared street concept also holds promise for the neotraditional development. Neotraditional supporters claim a highly interconnected street network (usually a grid) will reduce travel distance and time, and will extend accessibility by offering more route choices.[55, 56] Yet, increased accessibility on all the streets raises the likelihood of cut-through traffic and speeds inappropriate to residential neighborhoods—the original impetus for abandoning grids in favor of discontinuous street systems more than sixty years ago. Shared streets in a connected system can eliminate the deficiencies of the grid. Speeds will be reduced and through traffic by nonresidents discouraged, yet connective features such as access points and route choices will be much more numerous than in the typical hierarchical, discontinuous street system. This design would thus combine a high degree of livability and safety in the residential streets while maintaining links to the larger neighborhood.

Restoring a human scale to residential streets can benefit all, from the residents, to the developer, to the local authority. Developers would find that shared streets create an attractive public environment, thereby increasing the sales potential. Initiatives by manufacturers can further reduce installation costs and prompt developers to adopt the change. Cities and towns would then enjoy a durable street system that involves residents with their streets, and would therefore have fewer maintenance problems, as well as better traffic safety and control. Though residents have the most to gain from the shared street layout, they are probably the most ignorant of it as a workable alternative. Public information about shared streets is nonexistent, yet the involvement of neighborhood residents in planning and implementing traffic management is crucial for acceptance. Through improved information, publications, and grassroots professional involvement, the possibility of redesign can be introduced. Such processes initiated many of the suburban shared streets in The Netherlands and in Israel.

The shared street concept provides an opportunity for American planners and designers, as it did for their counterparts in Europe, to take the lead in finding alternatives to the typical suburban design. Residential streets are the least influenced by traffic. Their domain lies more in architecture than in engineering, and thus should be under the design jurisdiction of the architect, landscape architect, and planner. Application of this concept in new settings invites a variety of site configurations. Such designs can promote a community that is safer, child-oriented, and aesthetically more pleasing.

THE CASE FOR CUL-DE-SACS

The New Urbanists' advocacy of interconnecting street patterns underscores the historical debate between the grid system and the curvilinear discontinuous system. Neotraditional concepts rely on the Garden City ideal as represented by Unwin and his American counterparts, Perry and Stein. Yet these latter designers were strongly opposed to the interconnected street system as part of a residential development. Lewis Mumford claimed: "With a T-square and a triangle, finally, the municipal engineer could, without the slightest training as either an architect or a sociologist, 'plan' a metropolis, with its standard lots, its standard blocks, its standard street widths, in short, with its standardized comparable, and replaceable parts. The new gridiron plans were spectacular in their inefficiency and waste. By usually failing to discriminate sufficiently between main arteries and residential streets, the first were not made wide enough while the second were usually too wide for purely neighborhood functions . . . as for its contribution to the permanent social functions of the city, the anonymous gridiron plan proved empty."[57] Other critics suggest that the grid network system advocated in these new trends in subdivision design consumes more open space, is less supportive of an independent pedestrian network, and is less environmentally sensitive.[58]

Among many architects and planners, particularly the New Urbanists, the cul-de-sac street represents the ultimate building block of the suburban pattern: the disconnected formless pattern of "loops and lollipops" characteristic of much late twentieth-century suburban development. The term has become somewhat pejorative in environmental design for it represents the essence of suburbia today: the isolated, insular, private enclave, set in a formless sprawl of similar enclaves, separated socially and physically from the larger world, and dependent upon the automobile for its survival. According to the principles of *feng shui*, the ancient Chinese art of geomancy, cul-de-sacs are undesirable because they trap evil spirits; the house at the end of a cul-de-sac is thought to be particularly vulnerable to invasion. Although much despised by many leading architects and planners, it seems to be much loved by suburban residents and developers. This disagreement between the values of designers and the public needs to be examined.

Despite the criticisms, there is much to be said in favor of the cul-de-sac itself as a pattern for residential space, a form that has deep historical roots. What is a cul-de-sac? A French term, it means literally, "bottom of the sack." Commonly, it refers to a dead-end street, row, lane, or a square, quad, quadrangle, place, or yard. The *Oxford English Dictionary* defines it as "a street, lane, or passage closed at one end, a blind alley; a place having no outlet except by the entrance."[59] Thus, the term actually refers to a variety of physical configurations.

As discussed earlier, the cul-de-sac pattern has been strongly encouraged by traffic engineering and subdivision standards. In its typical manifestation, the suburban cul-de-sac is a relatively short street, usually less than 1,000 feet, serving up to 20 dwellings. It is terminated by a circular turn-around space large enough in diameter for service and emergency vehicles to turn around in, with a typical radius of 35 to 40 feet. Single-family houses, each with its own garage and driveway, usually line it on both sides and continue around the circle. Sidewalks and street trees may or may not be provided. The only way into and out of this cozy enclave is via the single cul-de-sac entrance, which joins onto a collector street that services other similar cul-de-sacs. In its ideal form, all houses in a subdivision are situated on cul-de-sacs, and none are placed on the busier and noisier collector streets. A close cousin of the cul-de-sac is the loop street, which is similar in that it discourages through traffic, since it goes nowhere other than to the homes along it. However, it has two access points, and thus is usually longer than the cul-de-sac. Both loops and cul-de-sacs are often found in the same development.

This "loops and lollipops" pattern of residential land development has been criticized on several grounds. Obviously, it lacks the interconnectedness of earlier development patterns like the gridiron. One must always leave the cul-de-sac and get onto a collector street to go somewhere. Route choices are minimal, so one is stuck using the same paths day after day. Also, since so much of the street infrastructure is devoted to semiprivate dead-end roads, a heavy load of connecting and through traffic is forced onto a relatively small collector and arterial system, which often results in overload during peak periods. For the pedestrian, walks can be long and boring, with inefficient connections to nearby destinations. The sense of being part of a neighborhood or town, with a clear structure and identity, is often lost because the through streets and treed corridors that connect places and that communicate the personality of a community are gone. What is left is a string of

The disconnected, formless pattern of "loops and lollipops" characterizes much late twentieth century residential development. Although disliked by many architects and urban designers, the cul-de-sac is a favored form of suburban residents and developers. It offers privacy and is removed from the hazards and noise of traffic. *(a: © William Garnett; b and c: © Landslides, Alex S. MacLean)*

dead-ends on faceless connectors that seem to weave aimlessly. The pattern as it has evolved is usually difficult to conceptualize because there is so little apparent structure, no unifying element, or clear describable pattern. Moreover, it is usually boring in its repetitiveness. One lacks the sense of being part of a whole, of being in a neighborhood or town that is truly one's own, with a sense of civic identity and spirit. Of course, grid pattern developments can suffer from monotony, as well, despite the clarity and connectedness of the pattern.

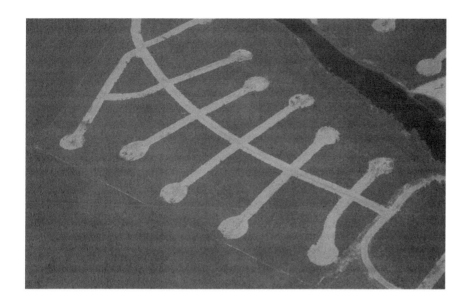

The cul-de-sac pattern, however, has several advantages that are worth considering. From the point of view of cul-de-sac and loop residents, the pattern offers quiet and safe streets, where children can play with minimal fears of the hazards of fast-moving traffic. A discontinuous short street system, unlike the grid, may promote neighboring, familiarity, and interaction.[60-63] Analysis of automobile accident data over several years supports the cul-de-sac and loop patterns as being more safe. Furthermore, a hierarchical discontinuous street system has been found to deter burglary rates compared with easily traveled street layouts, since criminals avoid street patterns where they might get trapped.[64] The troubled Five Oaks district of Dayton, Ohio was restructured to create several smaller neighborhoods by converting many local streets to cul-de-sacs. Within a short time traffic declined 67 percent and traffic accidents fell 40 percent. Overall crime declined 26 percent, and violent crime 50 percent. At the same time home sales and values increased.[65]

A recent comparative study of street patterns indicates significant user preference for the cul-de-sac and loop patterns for these reasons. Nine carefully selected California neighborhoods were examined in terms of safety performance and residents' perception of their street's livability.[66] The study neighborhoods represented different street layouts—grid, loop, and cul-de-sac—but were matched demographically. The findings suggest that cul-de-sac streets, and especially the lots at the end, perform better than grid or loop patterns in terms of traffic safety, privacy, and safety for play. Residents also preferred the cul-de-sac as a place to live, even if they actually lived on a through or loop street. People said they felt cul-de-sac streets were safer and quieter because there was no through traffic and it moved more slowly. They also felt they were more likely to know who lived on the street. One resident's comment was typical: "Our pets and kids are safer when there is a no-outlet street; you feel kidnapping is less likely—there is more of a sense of neighborhood." Thus, the study generally corroborated earlier transportation research on the values of a hierarchical discontinuous street pattern to residential areas. It also supported claims that cul-de-sacs are more frequently and more safely used by children.[67, 68] However, the cul-de-sac pattern was less preferred as an overall neighborhood pattern, and social interaction and neighborhood sense were not necessarily stronger on the cul-de-sacs. At the neighborhood scale, problems associated with cul-de-sac neighborhoods may stem more from land use issues than the street pattern itself. The single use zoning of most cul-de-sac neighborhoods results in poor access to schools, recreation, commercial centers, and jobs. Only rarely is there an interconnected pedestrian pathway system linking cul-de-sacs with adjacent streets, open spaces, and other neighborhoods.

The discontinuous street pattern is also supported by market demand. Home buyers often pay premium prices for the most isolated cul-de-sac lots.[69, 70] From the developer's perspective, the cul-de-sac pattern is popular, not only because it sells well, but also because the infrastructure costs are sig-

The residential court or lane of early American towns like Boston and Philadelphia provides the quiet and privacy of the suburban cul-de-sac, but with far more architectural distinction. This cobblestone lane on Boston's Beacon Hill is a prized residential location. *(© Michael Southworth)*

nificantly lower than for the traditional interconnected grid pattern, since there is up to 50 percent more road construction.

This is a dilemma for the designer committed to a more structured design. Might it be possible to satisfy both sets of needs: privacy, safety, and quiet, as well as connectedness, identity, and structure? The cul-de-sac certainly need not be an amorphous blob. The same benefits could be achieved with more architecturally defined and ordered patterns such as the courts, closes, and quadrangles in English and French villages of the Middle Ages, which Unwin emulated in his designs for Hampstead Garden Suburb. The residential court is also found in many early American towns, from Philadelphia to Boston. Today such spaces are usually prized locations for their sense of privacy, their intimate scale and charm.

It is possible to imagine a suburban residential environment based on such courts and closes, each a defined space with its own special character, and with limited automobile access, yet situated within an overall structure of boulevards and public spaces that contribute to the sense of being part of a larger community. While automobile movement would be controlled and limited to collector and arterial streets, pedestrian and bicycle circulation could have the kind of interconnectedness of the classic gridiron. The pedestrian network can parallel the vehicular ways, but can also connect cul-de-sacs and loops with each other, as well as with destinations such as parks, schools, and shops, creating a completely interconnected and efficient system.

The scheme used at Radburn is in fact a variant of this. Houses are clustered about automobile accessible cul-de-sacs. The pedestrian path system is expanded into greenways and parks, with paths connecting to each home, as

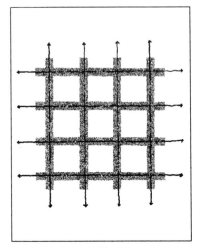

Conventional open gridiron

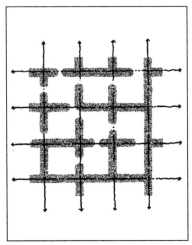

Gridiron with pedestrian connectedness and vehicular disconnectedness

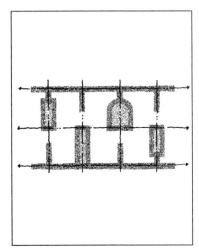

Connected cul-de-sacs and courts with public spaces

It would be possible to design new residential districts, and to retrofit old ones, to offer the best of both worlds: the interconnected pedestrian network and the limited access vehicular system. By connecting cul-de-sacs and loops with each other, and with neighborhood destinations, a walkable neighborhood can be created, while controlling the car. *(© Michael Southworth)*

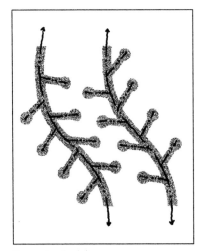

Conventional cul-de-sac pattern

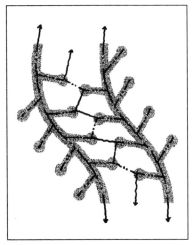

Pedestrian connected cul-de-sacs

Existing street grids can be retrofit with various types of barriers to divert through vehicular traffic. Berkeley, California has experimented with several techniques for limiting neighborhood traffic: planter-barriers, mid-street mini-parks, and bollards. *(© Michael Southworth)*

well as the school. Pedestrian connectedness is offered with minimal interference from the automobile. Although the open spaces at Radburn are rather lavish, the idea could be achieved with much less open space and focusing on the pedestrian pathway system.

Another example to consider is the retrofitting of traditional neighborhoods based on the interconnected grid found in most American small towns and streetcar suburbs built before the 1920s. These neighborhoods possess the connectedness, structure, walkability, and accessible land use patterns that many planners are seeking today in new residential developments. They are, however, subject to invasion by the automobile and often suffer from the noise and hazards that come with excessive traffic on local residential streets. Berkeley, California is one community that has attempted to deal with the problem. In effect, the grid system has been converted into cul-de-sacs and loops as far as vehicular circulation is concerned by placing traffic barriers in the form of planted areas or large concrete planters across the street at selected points. Pedestrians and bicyclists, however, can continue to use the interconnected grid. Originally an experiment, the scheme was strongly advocated by residents of participating neighborhoods, but was strongly disliked by outsiders who lost their through vehicular access. Nevertheless, support was broad enough to make it a permanent program.

Retrofitting an existing suburban cul-de-sac development to provide pedestrian connectedness would probably be more difficult. New pathways could be designed to interconnect cul-de-sacs, but in most cases they would have to be built on private land along lot lines. To acquire such easements is likely to be difficult, since residents are unlikely to give up a portion of their land and privacy, even though the sacrifice would be small. Moreover, in most suburban developments of this type, the land use patterns do not support connectedness—typically there is very little to connect besides houses.

127

Some suburban developments combine aspects of the cul-de-sac and shared street. Houses are clustered around paved and landscaped courts that serve both pedestrians and vehicles. *(a: Courtesy of Cornerstone Communities; b: © Eran Ben-Joseph; c: © Michael Southworth)*

Are walkable suburbs possible today? Perhaps the greatest need today is to shape new developments to support the pedestrian and bicyclist and to tame and confine the automobile. Although few neotraditional developments have been built thus far, the concepts have kindled an important debate on the future of residential development. By addressing and challenging current established street design standards and regulations, neotraditional concepts provide a platform for discussion between designers, planners, engineers, and residents. Traffic engineers, in particular, should acknowledge the need to review existing standards and to establish new frameworks that accommodate such trends. In February 1994 an ITE technical committee published *Traffic Engineering for NeoTraditional Neighborhood Design.*[71] While the report stops short of defining technical guidelines, it favorably reviews the features associated with neighborhood design. The report concludes: "To prepare for new NTND (NeoTraditional Neighborhood Design) developments traffic engineers should become aware of basic NTND concepts. Traffic engineers, as always, should be very concerned about safety, but they should be careful not to use safety as an excuse to avoid the consideration of what may actually be a good and safe neotraditional design. Engineers and others should recognize that NTND projects hold promise for a complex form of development which, if properly designed by all of the designers involved, can create very safe and livable new neighborhoods."[72]

Whether new urban development based on traditional patterns, the *woonerf*, or other models can be made to work in today's marketplace still remains to be demonstrated. The creation of walkable enclaves within regional sprawl, however delightful, may not reduce automobile dependence or solve regional transportation and environmental problems. To reduce automobile dependence it will be essential to begin to manage patterns of land use and transportation, while enhancing local livability. Without such thinking, piecemeal efforts to create imageable and comfortable streets and neighborhoods will result in little more than the old suburb in a new style. Local efforts at creating convenient, less auto-dependent neighborhoods and communities will be most effective within a regional framework that provides the transit infrastructure and encourages a denser pattern of development with mixed uses.

Tomorrow's Streets

Toward New Neighborhood Street Standards

The street, which is the public realm of America, is now a barrier to community life.

—Andres Duany

Street design standards in use today have a long history and their use has improved the safety, efficiency, health, and privacy of streets and neighborhoods. The problem is, while standards can of course help prevent the worst conditions, they can also stifle creativity and inhibit adaptation to local situations. What began as visionary design with valid motivations has often evolved into a rigid, overengineered approach. Once they are established, it is too easy to apply standards automatically.

As we have seen, the design and layout of residential streets have been increasingly regulated over the years. With the rapid rise in mobility and car ownership, engineers and planners have assumed streets were inadequate, resulting in standards that are often in excess of local neighborhoods' actual traffic requirements. These standards have then been imposed by local governments without allowing much flexibility. Thus, street standards have become deeply embedded in engineering and design practice, as well as in the legal and even the financial structures that support development. The results are all too visible in lookalike developments that are unresponsive to their users and to their geographic contexts. Local governments frequently have adopted standards mechanically following federal or state models, without considering the character and requirements of each project. Fear of liability has also helped embed such standards in codes as valid absolutes. As a result, modifications to old standards and completely new standards have been very slow to develop. Although some different approaches to road layouts have been tried, as in the work of neotraditional designers, institutionalized guidelines and standards have not changed. And since federal agencies have not advocated changes, lesser agencies are reluctant to do so. Local authorities see the federal guidelines as rules flatly recognized by all road-related groups, which clears them of all responsibility. Consequently, local planners and citizen groups rarely challenge existing street standards. Unconventional approaches to suburban layout face a nearly impossible barrier to approval.

Current problems in subdivision street design may be attributed to a single-minded focus on traffic control and a lack of integration between concerns for functional accessibility and livability. Residential street standards should be appropriate to street function, a function that is not only part of a transportation network, but also part of a residential community. Presently, all streets are defined in terms of their performance for traffic movement, but local or access streets should be considered more a part of a neighborhood environment than a transportation system. Residential streets are the least impacted by traffic. We must look at streets as complex community settings that serve a variety of functions—not simply as channels for moving traffic and emergency vehicles. Streets are also environments used for walking, bicycling, and jogging, for socializing, and for children's play. They are the staging spaces for community interaction and neighborhood development. As such, their design requires an understanding of social behavior, architectural and urban design, landscape architecture, and general planning. Their domain lies more in the design fields than in engineering. Thus, an argument can be made for placing residential streets under the design jurisdiction of architects and other environmental designers.

Architects, landscape architects, and planners can initiate the drive for improved residential streets. Designers need to work together with engineers to understand the multiple uses of streets and to place an emphasis on residents rather than vehicles, while acknowledging traffic patterns and street engineering. Developers too can be a driving force behind redesigning suburban layouts and the adoption of different street concepts. Residents have the most to gain in reevaluating street layouts and standards, yet they are probably the most ignorant of this viable alternative. The involvement of neighborhood residents in planning and implementing improved street designs is crucial for acceptance.

LIABILITY CONCERNS IN REEVALUATING STANDARDS

Until recently, public agencies have been reluctant to adopt new street designs and layouts. Engineering and public works departments, which have guided the development and management of residential streets, have often hesitated to adopt new traffic management schemes for fear of lawsuits by drivers, passengers, or pedestrians. However, the recent trend of neotraditional design, by challenging established standards and regulations, has stirred an important debate about the future of residential development that has extended to the transportation and civil engineering professions. In a recent nationwide survey of public works departments of 75 cities, more than half expressed willingness to reexamine their residential street standards and regulations. Furthermore, almost 70 percent of the cities were either taking or planning some traffic control measures in residential neighborhoods, and about 50 percent of the engineers surveyed knew of the shared street concept and its benefit to the residential setting.

Although many city officials have acknowledged the need to amend certain aspects of their regulations and create a more flexible framework for street design, most still think that the current practice is satisfactory. The survey indicated that a roadway width of 36 feet (11 m) is most widely used, and is considered to be the most appropriate dimension. Most of the respondents explained that this dimension is the best in allowing free traffic passage as well as on-street parking. In reality this width is not different from previously published guidelines, such as those by ITE and AASHTO.[1]

According to the same survey, liability and legal issues were cited as the most important drawback to implementation of different street configurations and traffic-calming measures. In order to avoid possible litigation cities often use a "worst case design scenario" as a yardstick for street width approval: cars parked on both sides of the street, an emergency vehicle with outriggers, and only one open travel lane leads to the requirement of excessive street width. Liability concerns are also reflected in the recent surge of private street construction. In many contemporary subdivisions developers try to utilize the private street option in order to minimize the required geometric design standards and cut down on their costs. Because the streets are maintained by the homeowner association, the city is typically exculpated from full liability. Thus, the city often permits their construction following less rigid standards, resulting in narrower roadways and smaller building setbacks. Almost all of the cities surveyed (84 percent) allowed for different street standard configurations in private developments. Among the cities that allow for construction of a narrower roadway, 64 percent required a minimum width of 20 to 25 feet (6–7.5 m). This width is often stipulated with special parking requirements, but it is still substantially less than the typical 36-foot (11 m) roadway width of the public street.[2]

It is important for city officials to realize that courts have usually ruled in favor of local jurisdictions that approved lower design standards for local roads, as long as the standards were set in writing.[3] This is an important point. Furthermore, in California, as well as in other states, under statutory "design immunity," a public entity is generally not liable for injuries caused by a dangerous condition of public property if three criteria are satisfied:

1. There is no causal relationship between the plan or design and the accident.

2. Approval of the plan or design prior to construction or improvement is only discretionary.

3. There is substantial evidence supporting the reasonableness of the plan or design.

As stated by the courts in several cases, this type of immunity reflects a legislative intent to insulate discretionary planning and design decisions by responsible public officials from review in tort litigation.[4] These acts are particularly important as liability and legal issues are cited by city transportation and public works departments as the most critical issue in implementing innovative street configurations and reduced standards.

LOCAL CONTROLS AND DESIGN INITIATIVES

The independence of local agencies and their ability to act independent of the government's yardstick is key to changing regulations and standards. In many parts of the United States such trends are beginning to emerge. As more communities are wrestling with quality-of-life problems due to uncontrolled growth, environmental pollution, and failure of existing infrastructure, they are beginning to assert their own power. Some of these communities are adopting management programs and devising local threshold criteria. Under such schemes, local objectives are translated into measurable limits for air quality, police and fire protection, parks and recreation, water, drainage, and traffic. Established thresholds may not be exceeded by new developments without proper mitigation or approval by the community.

The federal government has also acknowledged the importance of local decision making. An example of this can be seen in the federal Inter-Model Surface Transportation Efficiency Act of 1991 (ISTEA), which for the first time re-authorized distribution of the federal-aid highway and transit funds at the discretion of state and local agencies. This legislation shifts much of the transportation decision-making that has been under federal jurisdiction for more than four decades to states and cities. Local agencies, therefore, are free from binding regulations usually attached to federal funding, and are able to develop and support the programs and projects they see as appropriate for their communities.

This act opens the possibility for local communities to establish their own initiatives, and still be supported legally and financially by favorable agencies. For example, the city of Novato, California has recently adopted a new ordinance creating "rural street standards." These modified standards provide a tool that the city uses in workshop meetings with neighborhoods in order to arrive at reduced street designs. As stated by the ordinance: "The purpose of rural streets is to provide safe, convenient facilities for auto traffic, pedestrians, bicyclists, and equestrians and to maintain and restore the rural character of certain neighborhoods in, and adjoining, the City. These streets will be located generally in the more rural, non-urbanized areas of the City. For this reason, pavement widths within such streets will be reduced and the use of Portland cement concrete curbs, gutters, and sidewalks will be limited."[5]

Portland, Oregon is one of the few cities in the United States that is actively pursuing and changing their street standards. The Skinny Streets Program has been vigorously implemented in both established communities and new ones since 1991. By reducing local residential street width by as much as 12 feet (3.6 m), skinny streets have become a cost effective way to preserve livability and neighborhood integrity. Most streets are designed to be no more than 20 to 26 feet (6–8 m) wide depending on neighborhood parking needs.

Portland had been spending about a million dollars annually to install traffic calming devices because excessive street widths allowed for high speeds and cut-through traffic. Reducing the standards has not only improved the livability of the community, but has also reduced storm water runoff and the impact of grading on slopes, and has lowered costs.

The primary resistance to the Skinny Streets Program came from the Fire Department, which wanted unimpeded access to all neighborhoods. To overcome the opposition, the city decided to test the performance of existing 18

To overcome opposition to the Skinny Streets Program, the city of Portland tested the performance of existing 18- to 28-foot wide streets in older neighborhoods. The fire department was asked to drive their apparatus on these narrow streets while passing a parked bus and trucks. The results showed that these street widths provide adequate access for emergency vehicles. (© *Terry Bray, City of Portland*)

and 28 foot (5.5–8.5 m) wide streets in older neighborhoods. The Fire Department was asked to bring the apparatus they use and to show how these existing narrow streets make it impossible to do their job. The same was done with a dump truck and a bus. The results showed that these street widths provide adequate access for emergency vehicles. The Fire Department acknowledged that they could effectively serve narrow streets in residential neighborhoods that have access from either direction. They also agreed that they could serve cul-de-sacs which are less than 300 feet (95 m) long because, if blocked for any reason, fire personnel could carry needed equipment.[6]

The Skinny Streets Program has enjoyed a high level of support from both residents and government officials, and has generated much interest in other cities wishing to follow suit.

Other encouraging signs of less federal government involvement can be seen in the increasing role of the private sector in transportation-related issues and Transportation System Management (TSM) programs.[7] TSM programs provide developers with the opportunity to reduce a portion of their traffic-related subdivision requirements such as parking if they incorporate transit-related measures in their design. Such ordinances and tradeoffs have been applied in Sacramento, Seattle, and San Diego, with the most notable example being the subdivision of Laguna West near Sacramento. Obviously, there can be drawbacks to completely removing federal and state regulations, as well. If conditions result that are detrimental to health and safety—the very situation that spurred the need for government standards in the first place—actions would be needed to centralize regulations again.

SEMIPRIVATE STREETS
FOR FLEXIBILITY

In the near future the most probable avenue for implementing change in residential street standards and regulations may be in the private domain. Most cities allow for a different, more flexible set of standards to be implemented on private or semiprivate streets. In many developments, a homeowner association owns and maintains the streets as private streets, and often the local planning authority allows flexibility in their design. Because the local government has no legal responsibility for these streets, different configurations and standards can be introduced.

Streets in Forest Hills Gardens in Queens, New York are privately owned. Private streets allow residents and developers to establish their own design standards and relieve the municipality of liability. (© Michael Southworth)

Successful examples of this approach can be seen in the neotraditional developments of Seaside, Florida and Belmont, Virginia. In the private development of Seaside, the residential streets consist of one paved surface shared by pedestrians and cars. There are no raised sidewalks or curbs, and automobile speed is controlled by the narrow driving lane and the short street block. According to Andres Duany, one of the designers of Seaside, private streets do exempt the designer from many rules, but they still do not result in a true public domain like the European *woonerf* in either their spatial design

Since the streets of Seaside, Florida are privately owned, they could deviate from the established standards. One narrow paved surface, with no curb or raised sidewalk, is shared by pedestrians and cars. Cars tend to move slowly because of the narrow width and short blocks. *(© Peter Owens)*

or their civic characteristics. Duany's preferred method for avoiding the limitations of street regulations is to classify residential streets as parking areas, except for a few major streets designed as public. Designating an automobile area for parking exempts it from regular street standards and puts it under requirements that are usually more liberal and open to interpretation. Parking areas do not, for example, require building setbacks; their driving lanes are not controlled except for back-up space, and curb radii can be as small as 10 feet (3 m).[8]

Belmont was conceived as a planned unit development around 1988. The plan originally incorporated a curvilinear loop street system that conformed to the Virginia Department of Transportation's (VDOT) subdivision street requirements. In that same year, the Loudon County Board of Supervisors adopted a new initiative for neotraditional neighborhood design principles in response to the typical suburban development that had occurred over the last two decades in the region. As a result, the developer and the architectural/planning firm of Duany/Plater-Zyberk redesigned Belmont using the new principles. Yet, when the redesign was submitted, approval proceeded slowly due to the large number of variances requiring modifications to the zoning ordinance and subdivision guidelines.

Although the requested variances did not represent a drastic deviation from prevailing practice or typical ITE and AASHTO guidelines, their approval seemed unattainable. After prolonged and unsuccessful negotiations with VDOT, the developer proposed and received approvals for a private local street system to be maintained by a homeowner association. Only three collector and arterial streets were built to VDOT standards; the rest of the street system was placed in private hands. Belmont was the first development approved by the county that incorporated an extensive private street system.[9]

As a general approach to subdivision development, the privatization approach obviously is limited; it is difficult to imagine the bulk of residential streets being classified as "parking areas." But it can work in specialized or local situations like *woonerfs*, courts, or cul-de-sacs, where neighborhood access routes are part of a system separate from access to homes. The private street should only serve as a partial solution for changing standards for public streets. City officials should realize that the current practice of allowing a different set of standards on private streets acknowledges the inadequacy of their public street standards, and emphasizes that liability issues rather than actual performance guide change.

PERFORMANCE
STANDARDS VERSUS
SPECIFICATIONS

Typical standards for subdivision and street layouts like those issued by the FHA and ITE are specification standards, that is, they specify the exact physical features or the range within which they must lie. Performance standards, on the other hand, do not specify the exact size or shape, but rather what must be accomplished or avoided. They are a reaction to the rigidity of the traditional "Euclidean" approach to zoning regulations. Performance standards were first used to control industrial activity, for which rules specified permissible noise levels, smoke emissions, or water contamination. Rather than work by means of a predetermined physical plan or prototype, this form of regulation shapes the built environment by limiting the impacts of that change, leaving greater flexibility in design and construction. There is no one correct design or plan, but many possible solutions. It allows for a mixture of different types of solutions on a given site, where traditional specification standards tend to encourage uniformity. The adaptation of performance standards to zoning, subdivision, and street layout allows more flexible control. Working from a set of performance standards or criteria for streets, a vast number of alternative engineering solutions can be formulated to provide designs more suited to local conditions. This land use planning strategy encourages ecological sensitivity and more efficiency in the use of resources and land. It also provides an opportunity to adjust the construction cost to suit the socio-economic profile of the area.

The idea of performance standards is not at all new. In 1925 the U.S. Bureau of Standards in *Recommended Practice for Arrangement of Building Codes* stated:

> Wherever possible, requirements should be stated in terms of performance, based upon test results or service conditions, rather than in dimensions, detailed methods, or specific materials. Otherwise new materials, or new assemblies of common materials, which would meet construction demands satisfactorily and economically, might be restricted from use, thus obstructing progress in the industry. It is desirable that opportunity exist for establishing the merits of new or untried forms of construction. Compliance may be established by tests made under the building official's supervision, or by presenting evidence that the prescribed standards of performance have been met elsewhere under competent disinterested control.

The report goes on to say that copying of existing codes is an unwise practice:

> Sections or articles most emphatically should not be copied verbatim from other codes without careful study of their fitness; and particularly to determine if they conform to standards of uniformity recommended by the Department of Commerce. Many of the defects of existing codes result from this practice. The code from which sections are "lifted" may be an excellent one, but if the borrowing is not done with great care the result will be a disorganized accumulation of requirements, inconsistent with each other, and out of harmony with recent developments.[10]

These words apply not only to construction, but also to planning and site design. They are as valid today as they were over 60 years ago, yet the problem of inappropriate and rigid standards persists.

Performance zoning has been used in the small fishing village of Gay Head on the island of Martha's Vineyard off the coast of Massachusetts.

Conventional zoning seemed threatening and inappropriate to this quiet and rural village, which had no business or industrial district, and no staff to administer complex planning procedures. However, the town was seriously threatened with large-scale development of vacation homes. Residents wanted to retain the rural character, as well as the freedom from government controls they were accustomed to. The Gay Head Bylaw allows anywhere by right traditional uses such as single-family homes, schools, agriculture, fishing, and related small trades. Other uses are allowed anywhere, but only by permit, provided they satisfy certain performance conditions. Some examples of these performance conditions or standards include:

- "All outdoor parking, storage, loading, and service areas will be screened from the view of the public roads and from adjacent residences.

- There will be no odor, dust, fumes, glare, or flashing light which is perceptible without instruments more than 200 feet from the boundaries of the lot in question, except for warning devices, construction or maintenance work, or other special circumstances.

- Where possible, the site design will preserve and enhance existing trees over 12 inch caliper, water courses, hills, and other natural features, as well as vistas, ocean views, and historic locations, and will minimize the intrusion into the character of existing development."[11]

Another example of performance zoning can be seen in Bucks County, Pennsylvania. Faced with rapid suburbanization during the 1970s and inadequate tools to regulate development, the county set a new approach to control the form of suburban growth. Acknowledging the failure of traditional ordinances, the county challenged the "rigid control of lot sizes, setbacks, and housing types which often prevent the developer from using the most efficient design for a tract of land."[12] Through sets of diagrams and charts, Bucks County Performance Zoning dictates the factors that shape development including:

- Land use intensity, which is defined by density, open space ratio, and impervious surface ratio

- Site variables, which are defined by the site size, shape, and natural features

- Design variables, which are composed of different housing types (single-family, duplex, etc.)

A developer could then experiment with different scenarios applicable to the site, and by placing them in tables, could come up with several design configurations. The system allows for design flexibility and allows the developer to "request that certain standards be relaxed where this would be in keeping with good design practices, providing adequate light, air, privacy, fire protection, and other elements that design standards attempt to achieve."[13]

Although the performance standards focused mainly on general zoning regulations, they challenged and altered dimensional requirements. Variances were allowed for design standards such as lot width, building size, setbacks, parking requirements, and street width. In most cases major residential street widths were successfully reduced from 36 to 26 feet (11–8 m), and minor streets such as cul-de-sacs from 30 feet to 22 feet (9.2–6.7 m).

Such flexible planning and greater autonomy in local planning processes hold promise for the future, yet they do not guarantee success. Flexible models have sometimes failed in the past. The Cluster Housing and Planned Unit Development (PUD) of the 1960s, the most notable example of flexible sub-

THE LIMITATIONS OF FLEXIBLE PLANNING

Although the Planned Unit Development allows flexibility in street design and site planning, it tends to ignore the larger community. This collection of PUDs in the Bay Farm Island development of Alameda, California is almost a textbook of PUD approaches, but together they do not make a cohesive community. *(© Pacific Aerial Surveys)*

division layouts, allows latitude in the layout of street patterns, open spaces, and building sites. With their inward focus, there has been little concern with how a PUD development relates to the larger community. Moreover, they have often lacked cohesion and land use patterns have been homogeneous. Perhaps their most troubling consequence has been in the uncertainty they introduced to the local planning process. In an assessment of PUD practices, Jan Krasnowiecki, a lawyer involved in formulating the legal aspects of PUD developments, wrote: "My idea of PUD originally was that a procedure should be provided under which a municipality would be encouraged to throw away the book and sit down with the developer to negotiate a better product, hopefully a less expensive one for the consumer. I have a feeling this is not happening. The reason why this is not happening is that local officials do not like the responsibility that comes with a negotiated project, they prefer to find the answer in 'the book.'"[14] This statement, though made more than twenty years ago, still holds true in many of today's subdivision practices and particularly in street design.

SOME DESIGN CRITERIA FOR BETTER RESIDENTIAL STREET STANDARDS

What criteria should guide the development of new residential street standards? In tracing the evolution of residential street standards, a group of design issues has emerged that seem critical in the making of better residential streets. Several criteria are suggested here that can be used to evaluate existing residential streets and street standards, as well as to guide the making of new ones. These are intended to be flexible and responsive to local needs, rather than prescriptive solutions. They are meant to guide rather than impose, and should allow for development of creative solutions.

1. Support varied uses of residential streets including children's play and adult recreation. As residential streets are regularly used for play, recreation, and other social activity, their design should reflect a pedestrian orientation rather than just facilitate vehicular movement. As we have seen in the case of the *woonerf* or play street, it is quite possible to combine the social uses of streets with the needs of local traffic. At the same time street appearance can be enhanced through special paving, street furniture, play equipment, and integrated planting areas.

2. Design and manage street space for the comfort and safety of residents. Rather than focusing on the needs of automobiles, local residential streets should be designed with the needs of children, pedestrians, and bicyclists foremost. Motorists have highways and arterials where the car is king, but when entering a neighborhood, the automobile must be calmed. Layout, planting, and materials can help mitigate noise from traffic, as well as excessive heat, glare, and wind. Walking and playing surfaces should be comfortable, and appropriate furniture should be provided for the activities. In residential areas where signalized intersections are rare, T intersections or traffic circles are preferred since they are much safer than four-way intersections. Court or cul-de-sac layouts can provide the greatest amount of traffic safety, privacy, and area for safe play.

Residential streets should be designed for social uses as well as local traffic. *(© Eran Ben-Joseph)*

Streets should be designed and managed for the diverse needs of residents. Walking and playing surfaces should be comfortable, and appropriate furniture should be provided. *(© Donald Appleyard)*

3. Provide a well-connected, interesting pedestrian network. Since walking is more than a utilitarian experience, but is one that can be a joy, can contribute to good health, and can inform the walker about the community, pedestrian networks should also be designed to provide a pleasurable, informative experience. An ideal path system is explorable, offering surprises and new experiences, even after repeated use. The problems currently associated with cul-de-sac neighborhoods in existing suburbs stem as much from the land use pattern as from the street pattern itself. These land use problems can be seen in the lack of easy and convenient access to schools, shopping, and employ-

Pedestrian and bicycle networks should be designed for continuity and connectedness, even if the vehicular network is discontinuous. (© Eran Ben-Joseph)

ment. Another deficiency is the rare existence of an interconnected pedestrian pathway system linking cul-de-sacs with adjacent streets, neighborhoods, open spaces, and other destinations. Linkage in the overall neighborhood context is a quality that needs to be addressed if one is to use a discontinuous vehicular circulation pattern. Neighborhood designs often will benefit from the qualities associated with a dead-end street in the immediate surroundings of the dwelling, and the connective qualities associated with the grid in the larger context of the neighborhood. Clustering of dwellings around courts and cul-de-sacs should be supported with a well-connected subsidiary street and pedestrian system.

4. Provide convenient access for people who live on the street, but discourage through traffic; allow traffic movement, but do not facilitate it. The street system should provide access to all dwellings in a logical, coherent, and efficient way, and should maintain residents' ability to drive up as close as possible to their dwelling unit. Access to nonresidential activities such as shops, schools, and parks should be convenient, as well.

In interconnected street systems such as the gridiron, traffic control measures should be considered to eliminate extensive through traffic. If possible, these measures should be incorporated in the initial street design to create a coherent, harmonious scheme. Techniques include geometrical and physical changes in the street cross section and its physical appearance such as narrowing of the traffic lanes, elimination of the curbed sidewalk, change of paving materials, speed bumps, and extensive landscaping. Slow streets should incorporate a clearly defined area for slowing traffic at transition points between the collector and the local street, and street lengths should be short enough so that drivers will accept low speed driving conditions. Street design should correlate with actual traffic load. Typical traffic volumes on

The design of streets can enhance natural and historic features of the place. *(© Michael Southworth)*

residential streets should not exceed 1,000 vehicles per day, and 500 or less is ideal. Considering that the average vehicle trips generated by a single family in a detached home is 10.1 trips per weekday, 500 vehicle trips would translate to about 50 dwelling units.[15] Speeds should be below 20 mph (32 km), and drivers need to be educated to expect and accept the presence of children in the driving lanes.

5. Differentiate streets by function. Streets should be clearly distinguished within the network in terms of the functional differences between local residential streets and major collectors or arterials in the overall street design. This can be achieved in many ways. Landscape design can differentiate streets by use of thematic trees and other plants, and treatment of planting strips can vary according to street function. Major arterials may have a plant-

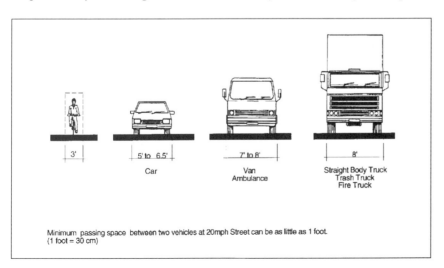

Minimum passing space between two vehicles at 20mph Street can be as little as 1 foot. (1 foot = 30 cm)

Street widths should be based on dimensions of the vehicles, rather than on preconceived notions of what is needed. Published standards are often excessive. *(© Eran Ben-Joseph after Devon Engineering Department)*

ed median strip, and local streets none. Similarly, sidewalk paving, width, and placement may vary. Street width, pattern, paving, parking treatment, and vehicle speed can be powerful indicators of function.

6. Relate street design to the natural and historical setting. Avoid generic design treatments and handbooks. Street designs should relate to and express the terrain, natural character, and historic traditions of the locale. Irregularities of the site—undulations, large rocks or trees, slopes, or other irregularities—should be incorporated rather than obliterated. Street details such as curb design, sidewalk paving, or street signs might relate to the regional vernacular, rather than being anonymous designs from a handbook or catalogue. Street designers should identify what is unique and special about the place and build a design that reinforces those qualities.

7. Conserve land by minimizing the amount of land devoted to streets. Several factors should shape the plan, including the design concept, actual needs for on-street parking, average traffic volumes generated by the abutting dwellings, and limitations arising out of the terrain. The street or area for vehicular movement should be based on dimensions of the vehicles themselves, rather than on abstract conceptions of what is needed. The width of the streets should be determined as part of the design process and should emerge as an integral part of the comprehensive architectural and planning concept. For traffic of up to 500 vehicles per day (i.e., servicing 50 to 70 dwellings), a single traffic lane is sufficient if parking lanes are incorporated, or passing spaces are provided. Similarly, corner radii are often excessive, and should be based on appropriate traffic speeds.

LOOKING AT COMMUNITY STREET STANDARDS

Are streets serving community needs? Communities need to evaluate their existing residential streets and street standards, as well as plans for new developments using criteria such as these. The process of assessing local streets and street standards can be a useful and engaging educational experience for both residents and city officials, as well as design and engineering professionals. Workshops might be held to show what has been done in other cities and the various techniques for managing traffic and reclaiming space for pedestrians. Neighborhood walks, discussion groups, and workshops can stimulate interest in reshaping local streets and involving residents in the process of planning and implementing changes.

Several techniques are useful, and most are relatively straightforward. A detailed and accurate map of street space can reveal how much space is devoted to streets. The addition of traffic volumes and movement patterns to the map will show whether the space is excessive in relation to use, whether the pattern discourages through traffic, and where there is excessive traffic. In the absence of traffic volume data, residents can easily do their own traffic counts. Observation of the use of street space at several times of day and week will show how well street space is serving the needs of children and adults for recreation and socializing. Conflicts between pedestrians and vehicles should also be noted. Interviews with residents are important in getting a sense of how comfortable the streets are for the people who live along them and to gain further information on user needs. These interviews can be supplemented with objective comfort measures such as night lighting, noise, wind, or temperature. A map of pedestrian space will show how interconnected the network is and how well it serves basic destinations. Neighborhood walks and photo surveys are useful tools, especially in thinking about the appearance of streets and pedestrianways. To understand the appropriateness of planting and landscape design along streets an inventory and map of plant materials and their condition is a starting point. Many communities have developed handbooks for selection of appropriate street trees and other street landscape materials, as well as their installation and maintenance so that residents can improve their own streets. In documenting safety, police accident records over a period of several years, as well as recollections of residents and maps of accident locations and traffic speeds are important.

We now need an interdisciplinary approach to street design and planning. Urban designers, planners, and engineers need to collaborate in developing new and revised standards that are more adaptable and responsive to the diverse users of streets and to varied social and geographic settings. The creation of street design standards should be an evolutionary process that incorporates multidisciplinary cooperation and results in flexible design guidelines suited to the context. Research on performance standards—their creation, use, and effectiveness—is needed to explore the possibility of stan-

THE WORK AHEAD

The diverse functions of local streets—walking, bicycling, driving, parking—can be designed efficiently and attractively without consuming excessive space, as illustrated in this street in Wassenaar, The Netherlands.
(© *Michael Southworth*)

dards that can respond to varied user needs and environmental values while also meeting basic requirements for safety. At issue is how to best design a residential street and how to advance new concepts in lieu of enduring rigid standards.

There are further questions that need to be addressed if traffic engineers are to accept unconventional street systems, including issues of safety, street performance, and travel behavior. We should reexamine the safety and traffic studies that generated street standards in the 1950s and 1960s, and should also compare safety performance and accident rates of suburban streets in relation to their specific layouts, particularly the discontinuous pattern versus the traditional gridiron. Residents' sense of traffic safety and their preferences for street layouts should be studied further. The relationship between accidents on residential streets and the street width, line-of-sight, and curvature needs to be further examined. If reduced standards can be shown not to increase hazardous conditions, a major constraint on street design would be eliminated. The typical hierarchical street layout should be examined; can a street hierarchy be created in a way that is different from recent and past practices? What are the effects of the local street pattern whether grid, hierarchical, or discontinuous, on driver behavior and local travel patterns?

Further investigation should be carried out on the relationships between social behavior and the street's physical form. Will reduced standards and different street configurations result in slower driving speeds and altered community behavior as they did in Europe? Would Americans value the benefits that arise from slower speeds and different street configurations? Or, as suggested by some, are American driving and living habits so different from those of Europeans that such changes could never take place?

A possible framework for researching these issues would be case studies of situations that have departed from conventional standards, as in privately owned streets and some neotraditional developments. Through what process were the standards revised? How well are the revisions working? Investigation of design prototypes and planning processes that have successfully changed street standards here and abroad can suggest ways of modifying guidelines in the United States. It is also worth looking at older neighborhoods, such as the streetcar suburb, that are based on different design assumptions. Another approach to answering these questions, although more difficult, would be to construct pilot projects in existing developments. Residents often complain about traffic problems on their streets and local authorities commonly install traffic control devices to mitigate these problems. In such localities, new standards could be set and streets could be redesigned as an experimental measure.

It is crucial that public and professional agencies and associations, such as the Institute of Traffic Engineers, the American Association of State Highway and Transportation Officials, and the National Committee on Uniform Traffic Laws and Ordinances, periodically review and revise their guidelines with input from environmental designers. The publication of such official documents provides the local jurisdictions with the necessary support to justify decisions contrary to conventional standards. General and public information concerning residential street design needs to be developed, as well. Most of what has been written on the subject has been published and circulated only in professional and academic settings.

Finally, professional schools have an important role to play in reshaping street standards and their use. The trend is toward increased professional fragmentation and separation. Today most architects and landscape architects have lost interest in the growing urban edge, and have almost completely forfeited their former role as large scale subdivision designers and planners to developers, builders, and engineers. At the same time, the profession of civil and road engineering is moving away from local design concerns into more abstract and large scale transportation system engineering. Civil and road engineers tend to focus on facilitating mass movement and are less likely to understand residential streets from the local point of view. A few schools, however, have begun to counter the trend by offering joint degree programs so that architects, landscape architects, planners, and engineers can acquire a common base of understanding and begin to work together. This movement should be encouraged.

The development of explicit yet variable standards for residential street design could open up new possibilities for subdivision street design that would induce users to alter their travel behavior, their choices of routes, and their modes of transportation. Street design with flexible standards increases the possibilities for different site planning configurations. Subdivision and lot arrangement can become adaptable and would not have to adhere to regulated shapes. Layouts can be more efficient and can provide a higher density without sacrificing the sense of openness. In theory, the developer can promote a community that is safer, child oriented, and aesthetically more pleasing. Street environments can then become a valuable asset for the development, just as they have been in Europe and Japan. A renewed effort to establish such guidelines through technical and official publications, as well as conferences, would provide a basis for change and legal backing for local planning agencies. At the same time, interim provisions should allow for alternative subdivision layouts that challenge existing standards and focus on habitat as well as movement.

It is now time to look at what has been created with a fresh eye and to rethink suburban street standards. This is a major task for designers, planners, and engineers in the years ahead.

Appendix A

Chronology of Events in the Development
of Residential Street Standards

312 BC Construction of the Appian Way begins

15 BC Emperor Augustus sets laws on street widths

300 AD The height of Roman military road construction

1485 Alberti designs ideal street

1550 The ideal Renaissance street is built: Strada Nuova, Genoa

1570 Palladio designs ideal street

1625 Earliest known paved American colonial city street, Pemaquid, Maine

1632 First highway law in North America, Commonwealth of Virginia

1747 First School of Bridges and Highway Engineering established, Paris

1765 London's Westminister Street improvement program

1775 Pierre-Marie-Jerome Tresaguet develops road construction method

1795 First American engineered road, Philadelphia to Lancaster toll turnpike

1816 John Loudon McAdam develops road construction method

1816 First American State Board of Public Works established in Virginia

1823 First American macadam road constructed in Maryland

1823 Park Village, Regent's Park, London, by John Nash

1824 First use of asphalt blocks in an urban setting, Champs-Élysées, Paris

1855 The "safety" bicycle invented in England

1869 Riverside, Illinois, Olmsted & Vaux

1875 Public Health Act; the "Bye Law" Street Ordinance, England

1875 Bedford Park, London

1877 First asphalt paving in North America: Pennsylvania Avenue, Washington, DC

1889 *Der Stadtebau*, Camillo Sitte

1892 State aid roads, New Jersey

1893 First American gasoline engine automobile tested in Springfield, MA

1893 First brick rural road, Ohio

1893 Office of Road Inquiry established, Department of Agriculture

1897 First Object-Lesson Road constructed, New Jersey

1898 *To-morrow: A Peaceful Path to Real Reform*, Ebenezer Howard

1902 *Garden Cities of To-morrow*, Ebenezer Howard

1903 Letchworth, England, Unwin & Parker, Architects

1905 Hampstead Garden Suburb, England, Unwin & Parker, Architects

1905 Office of Public Roads established, U.S. Department of Agriculture

1906 Bituminous macadam road, Rhode Island

1909 *Town Planning in Practice*, Raymond Unwin

1911 *The Width and Arrangement of Streets*, Charles Mulford Robinson

1916 Federal Aid Highway Act

1918 First federal aid road completed, California

1920 National Highway and Road Research Program established

1925 Adoption of Uniform Traffic Signs, Bureau of Public Roads

1927 Radburn, New Jersey, Clarence Stein
1929 *The Neighborhood Unit*, Clarence Perry
1930 Institute of Transportation Engineers established
1932 The President's Conference on Home Building and Home Ownership
1933 *The Radiant City*, Le Corbusier
1934 *The Design of Residential Areas*, Thomas Adams
1935 *Subdivision Development*, FHA-Title II of the National Housing Act
1936 *Planning Neighborhoods for Small Houses*, FHA
1938 *Planning Profitable Neighborhoods*, FHA
1939 *Subdivision Standards*, FHA-Title II of the National Housing Act
1939 Public Roads Administration established, Federal Works Agency
1939 *Standards for Modern Housing*, Public Health Association
1939 *Practical Standards for Modern Housing*, National Association of Housing Officials
1941 *Successful Subdivisions*, FHA
1947 *The Community Builders Handbook*, Community Builders Council and ULI
1947 *A Checklist for the Review of Local Subdivision Controls*, U.S. National Housing Agency
1948 *Planning the Neighborhood*, American Public Health Association
1949 Federal Highway Administration established
1952 *Suggested Land Subdivision Regulations*, U.S. Housing and Home Finance Agency
1953 *Neighborhood Standards for California*, FHA
1954 *A Policy on Geometric Design of Rural Highways*, American Association of State Highway Officials
1957 *Subdividing for Traffic Safety*, Harold Marks, Eno Foundation
1957 *A Policy on Arterial Highways in Urban Areas*, American Association of State Highway Officials
1961 *Geometrics of Local and Collector Streets*, Harold Marks, ITE
1961 *New Approaches to Residential Land Development*, Urban Land Institute
1961 *Building Traffic Safety into Residential Development*, Urban Land Institute
1962 *Suggested Land Subdivision Regulations* (revised), U.S. Housing and Home Finance Agency
1962 *Adopted Standards*, League of California Cities
1962 *Parking Dimensions*, Automobile Manufacturers Association
1963 Standard Practices for Street and Highway Lighting, American Standard Association
1965 *Traffic Engineers Handbook*, Institute of Traffic Engineers
1965 *Recommended Practices for Subdivision Streets*, Institute of Traffic Engineers
1968 National Committee on Uniform Traffic Laws and Ordinance

1970   *Design Guide for Local Roads and Streets*, American Association of State Highway Officials

1971   First *woonerf* constructed in The Netherlands

1974   *Residential Streets*, Urban Land Institute

1981   *Livable Streets*, Donald Appleyard

1983   Seaside, Florida, traditional neighborhood development, by Duany & Plater-Zyberk

1984   *Recommended Guidelines for Subdivision Streets*, ITE

1988   Kentlands, Maryland, traditional neighborhood development, by Duany & Plater-Zyberk

1989   *Residential Street Design and Traffic Control*, Institute of Transportation Engineers

1990   Laguna West, California, neotraditional development by Peter Calthorpe Associates

1991   *Intermodal Surface Transportation Efficiency Act*, Federal Highway Administration

1994   *Traffic Engineering for NeoTraditional Neighborhood Design*, Institute of Transportation Engineers

Appendix B

A Graphic Survey of Street Cross Sections

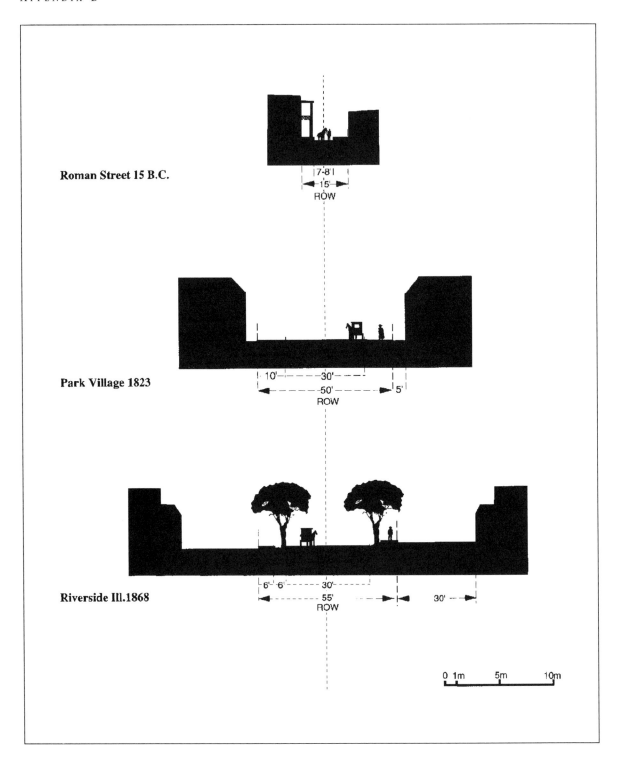

Roman Street 15 B.C.

Park Village 1823

Riverside Ill. 1868

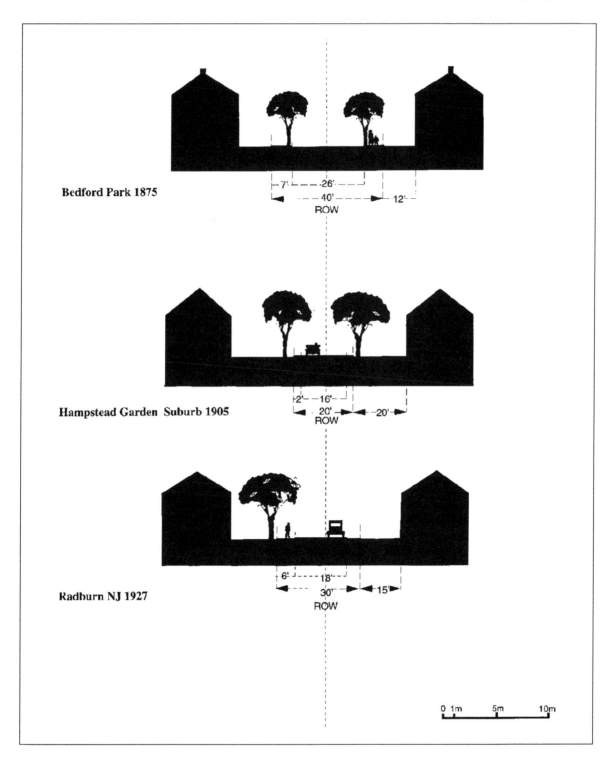

Bedford Park 1875

Hampstead Garden Suburb 1905

Radburn NJ 1927

0 1m   5m   10m

157

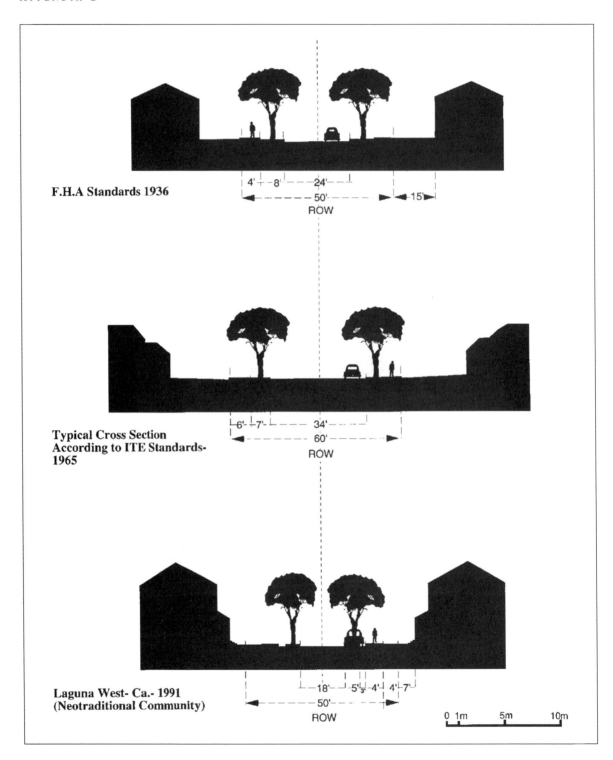

F.H.A Standards 1936

Typical Cross Section
According to ITE Standards-
1965

Laguna West- Ca.- 1991
(Neotraditional Community)

Chapter End Notes

Introduction

[1] Michael Renner, *Rethinking the Role of the Automobile* (Washington, DC: World Watch Institute, 1988).

[2] Mark Hanson, "Automobile Subsidies and Land Use," *Journal of the American Planning Association*, 58:1 (Winter 1992) 66.

[3] *1990 Highway Statistics* (Washington, DC: United States Department of Transportation, Federal Highway Administration).

[4] Institute of Transportation Engineers, *Recommended Guidelines for Subdivision Streets* (Washington, DC: ITE, 1967, 1984) 5–6.

[5] Sim Van der Ryn and Peter Calthorpe, *Sustainable Communities* (San Francisco: Sierra Club Books, 1986) 38.

[6] Ruth E. Knack, "Rules Made to be Broken," *Planning* 54:11 (1988) 16–22.

[7] Urban Land Institute, *Residential Streets: Objectives, Principles and Design Considerations* (Washington, DC: ULI, 1990) 20.

Chapter One

[1] *Vitruvius on Architecture*, trans. Frank Granger (Cambridge: Harvard University Press, 1931) Book I, Ch. VI, 53–61.

[2] Robert James Forbes, *Notes on the History of Ancient Roads and Their Construction* (Amsterdam: N.V. Noord-Hollandsche Uitgevers-MIJ, 1934).

[3] Forbes.

[4] Leon Battista Alberti, *Ten Books on Architecture*, 1485, trans. James Leoni, 1755, ed. James Rykwert (New York: Transatlantic Arts, 1966) Book IV, Ch. V, 75.

[5] Alberti, Book IV, Ch. V, 75.

[6] Andrea Palladio, *The Four Books of Architecture*, republication of the work first published by Isaac Ware in 1738 (New York: Dover Publications, 1965) Book III, Ch. II, 60.

[7] Charles Singer and E. J. Holmyard. *A History of Technology* (Oxford: Oxford University Press, 1958).

[8] Albert Rose, *Public Roads of the Past* (Washington, DC: American Association of State Highway Officials, 1953) 22.

[9] Walter Creese, *The Search for Environment: The Garden City Before and After* (New Haven: Yale University Press, 1966) 69.

[10] Creese, 76.

[11] Creese, 76.

[12] Lawrence Stone, *The Family, Sex and Marriage in England 1500–1800* (New York: Harper & Row, 1977).

[13] Robert Fishman, *Bourgeois Utopias: The Rise and Fall of Suburbia* (New York: Basic Books, 1987) 26.

[14] Letter to John Soane, September 18, 1822.

[15] Hermann Pückler-Muskau, *Tour in England, Ireland, and France, in the years 1828 & 1829* (London: Effingham Wilson, 1832) v. ii, 204–205.

[16] Andrew Jackson Downing, *The Architecture of Country Houses* (New York: D. Appleton and Company, 1850) preface.

[17] Olmsted, Vaux, and Co., *Preliminary Report Upon the Proposed Suburban Village of Riverside*, 1868, reprinted in S. B. Sutton, ed., *Civilizing American Cities: A Selection of Frederick Law Olmsted's Writings on City Landscapes* (Cambridge: MIT Press, 1971) 295.

[18] Kenneth Jackson, *Crabgrass Frontier: The Suburbanization of America* (New York: Oxford University Press, 1985) 75.

[19] Olmsted, Vaux, and Co., *Report Upon A Projected Improvement of the Estate of the College of California at Berkeley Near Oakland*, 1866, in Sutton, 265.

[20] Olmsted, Vaux, and Co., in Sutton, 284.

[21] Olmsted, Vaux, and Co., in Sutton, 292.

[22] Olmsted, Vaux, and Co., in Sutton, 300.

[23] Olmsted, Vaux, and Co., in Sutton, 301.

Chapter Two

[1] M. Moore, "Sanitary Oversight of Dwellings," *Charities Review*, 4:8 (June 1895) 438–439.

[2] Frederick Howe, "The Garden Cities of England," *Scribner's Magazine*, July 1912.

[3] Carol Aronovici, "Suburban Development," *Annals of the American Academy of Political and Social Science*, 51 (1914) 238.

[4] Walter Creese, *The Search for Environment: The Garden City Before and After* (New Haven: Yale University Press, 1966) 79.

[5] Creese, 82.

[6] T. Affleck Greeves, *Bedford Park: The First Garden Suburb* (London: Anne Bingly, 1975), figure 1.

[7] "Bedford Park, London," *Chamber's Journal*, 18 (31 December 1881) 840.

[8] *Daily News*, 5 May 1880 (London).

[9] Raymond Unwin, *Town Planning in Practice* (London: Fisher Unwin, 1909) 393.

[10] Unwin, 126.

[11] Ebenezer Howard, *Garden Cities of To-morrow* (London: Faber and Faber, 1902, 1945) 48.

[12] Howard, 1945 edition, 26.

[13] Unwin, 299.

[14] Howe, 5.

[15] Blake McKelvey, *The Urbanization of America (1860–1915)* (New Brunswick, NJ: Rutgers University Press, 1963).

[16] Charles Mulford Robinson, *The Improvement of Towns and Cities, or The Practical Basis of Civic Aesthetics* (New York: Putnam, 1902).

[17] Charles Mulford Robinson, *The Width and Arrangement of Streets: A Study in Town Planning* (New York: The Engineering News Publishing Company, 1911) 178.

[18]Robinson, 1911, 100–101.

[19]Robinson, 1911, 114.

Chapter Three

[1] John Rae, *The Road and the Car in American Life* (Cambridge, MA: MIT Press, 1971).

[2] Albert Rose, *Public Roads of the Past* (Washington, DC: American Association of State Highway Officials, 1953) 75–76.

[3] W. Stull Holt, *The Bureau of Public Roads: Its History, Activities and Organization*, Service Monographs of the United States Government, no. 26 (Baltimore: Johns Hopkins Press, 1923) 3.

[4] 27 Stat. L., 734, 737.

[5] Floyd Clymer, *Those Wonderful Old Automobiles* (New York: McGraw-Hill, 1953).

[6] Mark Sullivan, *Our Times: The United States 1900–1925*, Vol. III of *Pre-War America* (New York: C. Scribner's Press, 1930) 339–340.

[7] Rae, 32.

[8] Rose, 90.

[9] Institute of Government, University of North Carolina, *Popular Government*, 22 (December 1955) 1.

[10]Neil Postman, *Technopoly: The Surrender of Culture to Technology* (New York: Alfred A. Knopf, 1992) 51.

[11]Mel Scott, *American City Planning Since 1890* (Berkeley, CA: University of California Press, 1969).

[12]Christine Boyer, *Dreaming the Rational City, the Myth of American City Planning* (Cambridge: MIT Press, 1983) 60.

[13]Ann Christensen, *The American Garden City: Concepts and Assumptions*, diss., University of Minnesota, 1978, 95.

[14]Boyer, 144.

[15]Lewis Mumford, "The Intolerable City; Must it Keep Growing?" *Harper's Monthly* 152 (February 1926) 287.

[16]Mumford, 287–288.

[17]Clarence S. Stein, *Toward New Towns for America* (Liverpool: University Press of Liverpool, 1951) 23.

[18]Stein, 41.

[19]Stein, 47.

[20]Stein, 47.

[21]Stein, 44.

[22]Clarence Arthur Perry, *The Neighborhood Unit*, monograph in series: *Regional Survey of New York and Its Environs* (New York: Regional Plan Association, 1929) 34.

[23]In the 1920s regional and metropolitan concerns resulted in many large-scale planning efforts from coast to coast. The Boston Metropolitan Planning Commission was established in 1923. The Los Angeles

County Regional Planning Commission was established at the same time and focused on the needs for highways, water conservation, sanitation, zoning, and parks. In New York five regional planning bodies were established: the Niagara Frontier Planning Board, the Onondaga County Regional Planning Board, the Capitol District Regional Planning Association, the Central Hudson Valley Regional Planning Association, and the Regional Plan of New York and its Environs (Scott, 1969).

[24] Boyer, 184.

[25] New York Regional Plan Association, *Regional Plan of New York and Its Environs* (New York: NYRPA, 1929).

[26] Perry, 26–30.

[27] Le Corbusier, *The City of To-morrow and its Planning*, 1929, trans. Frederick Etchells (New York: Dover Publications, 1987) 19.

[28] Le Corbusier, 38.

[29] Le Corbusier, 10–12.

[30] Le Corbusier, 208.

[31] Le Corbusier, 124.

[32] Ludwig Hilberseimer, *The New Regional Pattern; Industries and Gardens, Workshops and Farms* (Chicago: Paul Theobald, 1949) 137.

[33] Le Corbusier, 123.

[34] Rae, 38.

[35] Rae, 74.

[36] Institute of Transportation Engineers, "A Retrospective," *Institute of Transportation Engineers Journal*, 50:8 (1980) 11.

[37] Institute of Transportation Engineers, 1980.

[38] Theodore Matson and Wilbur Smith, *Traffic Engineering* (New York: McGraw-Hill, 1955) 3.

[39] Matson and Smith, 410.

Chapter Four

[1] Federal Housing Administration (FHA), *The FHA Story in Summary, 1934–1959* (Washington, DC: FHA, 1959).

[2] President's Conference on Home Building and Home Ownership, *Slums, Large Scale Housing and Decentralization—Conference Proceedings* (Washington, DC: National Capital Press, 1932).

[3] Clarence Arthur Perry, "The Neighborhood Unit," *Regional Plan of New York and Its Environs* (New York: Regional Plan Association, 1929).

[4] Adams incorporated much of this manuscript in a later book, *The Design of Residential Areas* (Cambridge, MA: Harvard University Press, 1934).

[5] John Gries and James Ford, eds., *Planning for Residential Districts: Report on the President's Conference on Home Building and Home Ownership* (Washington, DC: National Capitol Press, 1932) 71.

[6] Franklin D. Roosevelt, "Back to the Land," *Review of Reviews,* 84 (October 1931) 63–64.

[7] John Rae, *The Road and the Car in American Life* (Cambridge, MA: MIT Press, 1971) 225.

[8] Clarence S. Stein, *Toward New Towns for America* (Liverpool: University Press of Liverpool, 1951) 119–124.

[9] *The Regional Plan of the Philadelphia Tri-State District* (Philadelphia: Regional Planning Federation of the Philadelphia Tri-State District, 1932) 1.

[10] New York Regional Plan Association, *Regional Plan of New York and Its Environs* (New York: NYRPA, 1929) 18.

[11] FHA, 1959, 12.

[12] Marc Weiss, *The Rise of the Community Builder* (New York: Columbia University Press, 1987).

[13] Weiss, 152.

[14] FHA, *Subdivision Development: Standards for the Insurance of Mortgages on Properties Located in Undeveloped Subdivisions* (Washington, DC: FHA, 1935) Circular no. 5, January 10.

[15] These standards and the succeeding ones are based on the following major FHA standard setting publications: *Subdivision Development,* Circular no. 5, January 10, 1935; *Planning Neighborhoods for Small Houses,* Technical Bulletin no. 5, July 1, 1936; *Subdivision Standards,* Circular no. 5, May 1, 1937 (Revised August 15, 1938 and September 1, 1939); *Planning Profitable Neighborhoods,* Technical Bulletin no. 7, 1938; *Principles of Planning Small Houses,* Technical Bulletin no. 4, July 1, 1940 (updated issue of the 1936 publication, revised June 1, 1946); *Successful Subdivision,* Land Planning Bulletin no. 1, March, 1941.

[16] FHA, *Planning Neighborhoods for Small Houses,* Technical Bulletin no. 5 (Washington, DC: FHA, July 1, 1936).

[17] FHA, 1936, 12.

[18] Weiss, 153.

[19] Harold W. Lautner, *Subdivision Regulation: An Analysis of Land Subdivision Control Practices* (Chicago: Public Administration Service, 1941) 1.

[20] Lautner, 113.

[21] International City Managers Association, *Local Planning Administration, Municipal Management Series* (Chicago: ICMA, 1941) 256.

[22] Lautner, 117.

[23] Urban Land Institute (ULI), *The Community Builders Handbook* (Washington, DC: ULI, 1947) 7.

[24] ULI, 1947, 62.

[25] ULI, 1947.

[26] ULI, *Building Traffic Safety Into Residential Development* (Washington, DC: ULI, 1961).

[27]ULI, *New Approaches to Residential Land Development*, Technical Bulletin no. 40 (Washington, DC: ULI, 1961).

[28]ULI, *Residential Streets: Objectives, Principles and Design Considerations* (Washington, DC: ULI, 1974, 1990).

[29]National Association of Home Builders, *Home Builders Manual for Land Development* (Washington, DC: NAHB, 1950) 114–118.

[30]Harold Marks, "Subdividing for Traffic Safety," *Traffic Quarterly,* 11:3 (July 1957) 308–325.

[31]Marks, "Geometrics of Local and Collector Streets," in *ITE Proceedings, 31st Annual Meeting* (Washington, DC: ITE, 1961) 105–116.

[32]Institute of Transportation Engineers (ITE), *Recommended Guidelines for Subdivision Streets* (Washington, DC: ITE, 1965, 1984).

[33]ITE, "Guidelines for Residential Subdivision Street Design," *Institute of Transportation Engineers Journal,* 60:5 (1990) 35–36.

Chapter Five

[1] Clarence S. Stein, *Toward New Towns for America* (Liverpool: University Press of Liverpool, 1951) 42.

[2] Calthorpe Associates with Mintier & Associates, *Transit-Oriented Development Design Guidelines* (Sacramento County Planning & Community Development Department, November 1990) 5.

[3] Stephen P. Gordon and J. B. Peers, *Designing a Community for TDM: The Laguna West Pedestrian Pocket* (Washington, DC: 71st Annual Meeting of the Transportation Research Board, 1991).

[4] Michael McNally and Sherry Ryan, *A Comparative Assessment of Travel Characteristics for NeoTraditional Development* (University of California, Irvine: Institute of Transportation Studies, 1992).

[5] Martin J. Wells, *Neo-Traditional Neighborhood Development: You Can Go Home Again* (Arlington, Virginia: Wells & Assoc., Inc., 1993).

[6] Walter Kulash, "Traditional Neighborhood Development: Will the Traffic Work?" (Bellevue, WA: Eleventh International Pedestrian Conference, 1990).

[7] McNally and Ryan.

[8] Richard K. Untermann, "Accommodating the Pedestrian: Adapting Towns and Neighborhoods for Walking and Bicycling," in *Personal Travel in the US, Volume II, A Report of the Findings from 1983–1984 NPTS, Source Control Programs* (Washington, DC: United States Department of Transportation, 1990).

[9] Gerald Barber, "Aggregate Characteristics of Urban Travel," in *The Geography of Urban Transportation*, Susan Hanson, ed. (New York: The Guilford Press, 1986) 73–90.

[10]Kiyoshi Ichikawa, Kioshi Tanaka, and Hirotada Kamiya, "Living Environment and Design of 'Woonerf,'" *International Association of Traffic and Safety Sciences*, 8 (1984) 40–51.

[11] Abishai Polus, *Evaluation of the Characteristics of Shared Streets*, Report no. 85-72 (Haifa, Israel: Transportation Research Institute, 1985).

[12] Joop H. Kraay, "Woonerfs and other Experiments in the Netherlands," *Built Environment* (1986) 12:1/2, 20–29.

[13] Brenda Eubank, "A Closer Look at the Users of Woonerven," in *Public Streets for Public Use*, ed. Ann Vernez Moudon (New York: Van Nostrand, 1987) 63–79.

[14] Ulla Engel, *Effects of Speed Reducing Measures in Denish Residential Areas*, Proceedings of Conference on Road Safety and Traffic Environment in Europe (Gothenburg, Sweden, September 1990) 95–135.

[15] Carmen Hass-Klau, Inge Nold, Geert Böcker, and Graham Crampton, *Civilized Streets: A Guide to Traffic Calming* (Brighton, England: Environmental and Transport Planning, 1992).

[16] Colin Buchanan, ed., *Traffic in Towns: A Study of the Long Term Problems of Traffic in Urban Areas* (London: Minister of Transport, Her Majesty's Stationery Office, 1963).

[17] Carmen Hass-Klau, *The Pedestrian and City Traffic* (London: Belhaven Press, 1990).

[18] Buchanan.

[19] Hass-Klau, 1990.

[20] Peter Jonquiére, *Woonerf: An Environment for Man and Transport Together—The Present Aspects*, Second International Symposium on Man and Transport—The Future Aspects (Tokyo, Japan, 1978).

[21] Hass-Klau, 1990.

[22] Ministry of Transport and Public Works, *Woonerven—Minimum Design Standards and Traffic Regulation*, RVV no. 179 (The Hague, The Netherlands: Ministry of Transport and Public Works, 1976).

[23] Jonquiére.

[24] *Hosha Kyozendoro no Rinen to Jisen*, (Pedestrian and Automobile Coexistence on Residential Streets—Theory and Practice) (Tokyo, Japan: Toshi Jutaku Henshubu, 1983).

[25] Warner Brilion and Harold Blanke, *Traffic Safety Effects from Traffic Calming*, Proceedings of Conference on Road Safety and Traffic Environment in Europe (Gothenburg, Sweden, September 1990) 135–148.

[26] Rodney Tolley, *Calming Traffic in Residential Areas* (Great Britain: Brefi Press, 1990).

[27] Carmen Hass-Klau, 1992.

[28] Kenneth Kjemtrup and Lene Herrstedet, "Speed Management and Traffic Calming in Urban Areas in Europe: A Historical View," *Accident Analysis and Prevention* (Special Issue), 24:1 (1992) 57–66.

[29] "Roads for People and Cars: Considerations for Residential Areas," *The Wheel Extended—Toyota Quarterly Journal*, 73 (1992).

[30]Eran Ben-Joseph, "Changing the Suburban Street Scene: Adapting of the Shared Street (Woonerf) Concept to the Suburban Environment," *Journal of the American Planning Association*, 61:44 (Autumn 1995).

[31]Department of the Environment, *Residential Roads and Footpaths*, Bulletin no. 32 (London, England: Department of the Environment, Her Majesty's Stationery Office, 1977, 1992).

[32]Eubank.

[33]Ichikawa.

[34]Polus, 1985.

[35]Abishai Polus and Joseph Craus, *Evaluation of Characteristics and Recommended Guidelines for Shared Streets*, Research Report no. 90-150 (Haifa: Technion-Israel Institute of Technology, 1990).

[36]Kraay, 1986.

[37]Joop H. Kraay, M.P.M. Mathijssen, and F.C.M. Wegman, *Towards Safer Residential Areas* (Leidschendam, The Netherlands: Institute for Road Safety Research (SWOV), 1985).

[38]Brilion and Blanke, 135–148.

[39]Ulla Engel.

[40]Department of the Environment.

[41]*Hosha Kyozendoro no Rinen to Jisen.*

[42]N. Kanzaki, Y. Ohomori, and S. Ishimura, *The Use of Interlocking Block Pavements for the Reduction of Traffic Accidents*, Second International Conference on Concrete Block Paving (Delft, Holland: April 1984) 200–206.

[43]Polus, 1985.

[44]Kraay, 1986.

[45]Julianne Krause, "Experience, Problems and Strategies with Area-Wide 'Verkehrsberuhigung'; Six Demonstration Projects," *Planning and Transport Research and Computation, Proceedings of Road Safety Meeting* (Sussex, England, July 1986) 284.

[46]John Nobel and M. Jenks, *Safety and Security in Private Sector Housing Schemes: A Study of Layout Considerations* (London: Housing Research Foundation, 1989).

[47]Brilion and Blanke.

[48]Engel.

[49]Janssen.

[50]Janssen.

[51]Kanazaki.

[52]Liz Beth and Tim Pharoah, *Adapting Residential Roads for Safety and Amenity* (London, England: South Bank Polytechnic, Department of Town Planning, 1988).

[53]Thomas Adams, *The Design of Residential Areas* (Cambridge, MA: Harvard University Press, 1934).

[54]Wolf Homburger, Elizabeth Deakin, and Peter Bosselmann, *Residential Street Design and Traffic Control* (Washington, DC: ITE, Prentice-Hall, 1989).

[55] Kulash.

[56] McNally and Ryan.

[57] Lewis Mumford, *The City in History: Its Origins, Its Transformations, and Its Prospects* (New York: Harcourt, Brace, Jovanovich, 1961) 48.

[58] Sam Kaplan, "The Holy Grid: A Skeptic's View," *Planning*, 59 (November 1990).

[59] *Oxford English Dictionary* (New York: Oxford University Press, 1989).

[60] H. Sanoff and J. Dickerson, "Mapping Children's Behavior in a Residential Setting," *Journal of Architectural Education*, 25:4 (1971).

[61] Barry Smith, "Cul-de-Sac Means Safety, Privacy for Home Buyer," *The Atlanta Journal and Constitution* (January 14, 1973, Section H).

[62] Donald Appleyard, *Livable Streets* (Berkeley, CA: University of California, 1981).

[63] Hae-Seong Je, "Urban Residential Streets: A Study of Street Types and Their Territorial Performances," diss., University of Pennsylvania (1986).

[64] J. Mayo, "Suburban Neighboring and the Cul-de-Sac Street," *Journal of Architectural Research*, 7:1 (1979).

[65] Oscar Newman, "Defensible Space—A New Physical Planning Tool for Urban Revitalization," *Journal of the American Planning Association*, 61:2 (Spring 1995) 149–155.

[66] Eran Ben-Joseph, *Livability and Safety of Suburban Street Patterns: A Comparative Study* (Berkeley, CA: Institute of Urban and Regional Development, University of California, Working Paper 641, 1995).

[67] Sanoff and Dickerson.

[68] Eubank.

[69] Smith.

[70] Lloyd W. Bookout, "Neotraditional Town Planning: Bucking Conventional Codes and Standards," *Urban Land* (April 1992) 18–25; "Neotraditional Town Planning: The Test of the Marketplace," *Urban Land* (June 1992) 12–17.

[71] Institute of Transportation Engineers (ITE), *Traffic Engineering for Neo-Traditional Neighborhood Design* (Washington, DC: ITE, 1994).

[72] ITE, 1994, 15.

Chapter Six

[1] Eran Ben-Joseph, *Residential Street Standards and Neighborhood Traffic Control: A Survey of Cities' Practices and Public Officials' Attitudes*, Working Paper 95-1 (Berkeley, CA: Institute of Transportation Studies, University of California at Berkeley, 1995).

[2] Ben-Joseph.

[3] C. R. Mercier, "Low Volume Roads: Closure and Alternative Uses," *Transportation Research Record*, 898 (1983) 110–115; "Cases for

Variable Design Standards for Secondary Roads," *Journal of Transportation Engineering*, 113:2 (1987) 181.

[4] Lawrence M. Freiser, ed., *California Government Tort Liability Practice* (Berkeley, CA: Continuing Education of the Bar, 1992) 367–372.

[5] Novato, California (City of), Rural Street Standards, Ordinance 1313 (July 12, 1994).

[6] Terrence L. Bray and Karen Carlson Rabiner, *Report on New Standards for Residential Streets in Portland, Oregon* (Portland, OR: Bureau of Transportation Engineering, 1991, revised 1994).

[7] Elizabeth Deakin, "Private Sector Roles in Urban Transportation," *ITS Review,* 8:1 (1984) 4–8; "Land Use and Transportation Planning in Response to Congestion Problems: A Review and Critique," *Transportation Research Record*, 1237 (1989) 77–86.

[8] Telephone interview with Andres Duany, 1994.

[9] Martin J. Wells, *Neo-Traditional Neighborhood Development: You Can Go Home Again* (Arlington, Virginia: Wells & Assoc., Inc., 1993).

[10] U. S. Bureau of Standards, *Recommended Practice for Arrangement of Building Codes* (Washington, DC: Bureau of Standards, 1925) 19.

[11] Kevin Lynch and Philip Herr, "Performance Zoning: The Small Town of Gay Head Tries It," in *City Sense and City Design*, ed. Tridib Banerjee and Michael Southworth (Cambridge: MIT Press, 1990).

[12] Bucks County Planning Commission, *Performance Zoning* (Bucks County, PA: Bucks County Planning Commission, 1973).

[13] Bucks County, 43.

[14] Jan Z. Krasnowiecki, "Legal Aspects of Planned Unit Development in Theory and in Practice," *Frontiers of Planned Unit Development: A Synthesis of Expert Opinion*, ed. Robert W. Burchell (New Brunswick, NJ: Center for Urban Policy Research, Rutgers University, 1973) 107.

[15] Institute of Transportation Engineers, *Trip Generation* (Washington, DC: Institute of Transportation Engineers, 1987).

Other References

Aitken, Thomas. 1907. *Road Making and Maintenance*. London: Charles Griffin and Company.

American Association of State Highway Officials. 1954, 1965. *A Policy on Geometric Design of Rural Highways*. Washington, DC: AASHO.

———. 1957. *A Policy on Arterial Highways in Urban Areas*. Washington, DC: AASHO.

———. 1984. *Design Guide for Local Roads and Streets*. Washington, DC: AASHO.

American Automobile Association. 1940. *Parking and Terminal Facilities*. Washington, DC: AAA.

———. 1946. *Parking Manual: How to Solve Community Parking Problems*. Washington, DC: AAA.

American Public Health Association, Committee on Hygiene of Housing. 1948, 1960. *Planning the Neighborhood*. New York: APHA.

Anderson, Stanford, ed. 1978. *On Streets*. Cambridge, MA: MIT Press.

Appleyard, Donald. 1981. *Livable Streets*. Berkeley: University of California.

Barber, H. L. 1917. *Story of the Automobile—Its History and Development from 1760 to 1917*. Chicago: A.J. Munson & Co.

Borth, Christy. 1969. *Mankind on the Move*. Washington, DC: Automotive Safety Foundation.

Boyer Christine. 1983. *Dreaming the Rational City, the Myth of American City Planning*. Cambridge, MA: MIT Press.

Brindle, R. E. 1991. "Traffic Calming in Australia: A Definition and Commentary," *Australian Road Research* 21, 2: 37–53.

Calthorpe, Peter and Sim Van der Ryn. 1986. *Sustainable Communities: A New Design Synthesis for Cities, Suburbs and Towns*. San Francisco: Sierra Club Books.

Calthorpe, Peter. 1993. *The Next American Metropolis: Ecology, Community, and the American Dream*. New York: Princeton Architectural Press.

Cervero, Robert. 1986. *Suburban Gridlock*. New Brunswick, NJ: Center for Urban Policy Research, Rutgers University.

———. 1991. "Congestion Relief: The Land Use Alternative," *Journal of Planning Education and Research* 10, 2: 119–121.

Conservation Law Foundation. 1995. *Take Back Your Streets*. Boston, Rockland, ME, and Montpelier, VT: CLF.

Creese, Walter. 1966. *The Search for Environment: The Garden City Before and After*. New Haven, CT: Yale University Press.

———, ed. 1967. *The Legacy of Raymond Unwin: A Human Pattern for Planning*. Cambridge, MA: MIT Press.

Dahir, James. 1947. *The Neighborhood Unit Plan: Its Spread and Acceptance*. New York: Russell Sage Foundation.

Devon County Council. 1991. *Traffic Calming Guidelines*. Devon: Devon County Council.

Duany, Andres and Elizabeth Plater-Zyberk. 1991. *Towns and Town-Making Principles*, Alex Krieger and William Lennertz, eds. Cambridge, MA: Harvard Graduate School of Design; New York: Rizzoli.

———. 1992. "The Second Coming of the American Small Town," *Wilson Quarterly* (Winter) 19–48.

Easterling, Keller and David Mohney, eds. 1991. *Seaside: Making a Town in America*. New York: Princeton Architectural Press.

Federal Housing Administration (FHA). 1938. *Principles of Land Subdivision and Street Layout*. Washington, DC: FHA.

Fischler, Raphael. 1993. *Standards of Development*. Dissertation, University of California, Berkeley.

Fishman, Robert. 1977. *Urban Utopias in the Twentieth Century: Ebenezer Howard, Frank Lloyd Wright, and Le Corbusier*. New York: Basic Books.

———. 1987. *Bourgeois Utopias: The Rise and Fall of Suburbia*. New York: Basic Books.

Forbes, R. J. 1934. *Notes on the History of Ancient Roads and Their Construction*. Amsterdam: N.V. Noord-Hollandsche Uitgevers-MIJ.

Garreau, Joel. 1991. *Edge City: Life on the New Frontier*. New York: Doubleday.

Gehl, Jan. 1987. *Life Between Buildings: Using Public Space*. New York: Van Nostrand Reinhold.

Gordon, Stephen P., John B. Peers, and Fehr & Peers Associates. January 1991. *Designing A Community for TDM: The Laguna West Pedestrian Pocket*. Washington, DC: Transportation Research Board.

Gregory, J. W. 1932. *The Story of the Road*. New York: The Macmillan Company.

Hall, Peter. 1988. *Cities of Tomorrow*. Oxford, UK: Blackwell.

Hanson, Susan, ed. 1986. *The Geography of Urban Transportation*. New York: Guilford Press.

Hegemann, Werner and Elbert Peets. 1922. *The American Vitruvius: An Architect's Handbook of Civic Art*. New York: Architectural Book Publishing Co.

Hilberseimer, Ludwig. 1944. *The New City*. Chicago: Paul Theobald.

Housing and Home Finance Agency. 1960. *Suggested Land Subdivision Regulations*. Washington, DC: HHFA.

Institute of Transportation Engineers. 1965–90. *Traffic Engineers Handbook*. Washington, DC: ITE.

Jackson, John Brinckerhoff. 1984. *Discovering The Vernacular Landscape*. New Haven, CT: Yale University Press.

———. 1994. *A Sense Of Place, A Sense of Time*. New Haven, CT: Yale University Press.

Jackson, Kenneth. 1987. *Crabgrass Frontier: The Suburbanization of America*. New York: Oxford University Press.

Jacobs, Allan. 1994. *Great Streets*. Cambridge, MA: MIT Press.

Jacobs, Jane. 1961. *The Death and Life of the Great American Cities*. New York: Random House.

Katz, Peter. 1993. *The New Urbanism: Toward an Architecture of Community*. New York: McGraw-Hill.

Kelbaugh, Doug, ed., et al. 1989. *The Pedestrian Pocket Book: A New Suburban Design Strategy*. New York: Princeton Architectural Press.

Kending, Jane, Susan Connor, Cranston Byrd, and Judy Heyman. 1980. *Performance Zoning*. Washington, DC: Planners Press.

Kostof, Spiro. 1991. *The City Shaped: Urban Patterns and Meanings through History*. Boston: Little, Brown.

———. 1992. *The City Assembled: The Elements of Urban Form through History*. Boston: Little, Brown.

Kraay, Joop H. 1987. *Safety in Residential Areas: The European Viewpoint*. Leidschendam, The Netherlands: Institute for Road Safety Research (SWOV).

———. 1989. *Safety Aspects of Urban Infrastructure: From Traffic Humps To Integrated Urban Planning*. Leidschendam, The Netherlands: Institute for Road Safety Research (SWOV).

Kunstler, James Howard. 1993. *The Geography of Nowhere: The Rise and Decline of America's Man-made Landscape*. New York: Simon & Schuster.

Lautner, Harold W. 1941. *Subdivision Regulation: An Analysis of Land Subdivision Control Practices*. Chicago: Public Administration Service.

Le Corbusier. 1933. *The Radiant City*, trans. Pamela Knight, Eleanor Levieux, and Derek Coltman. New York: Orion Press, 1967.

Lynch, Kevin. 1981. *Good City Form*. Cambridge MA: MIT Press.

Marks, Harold. 1957. "Subdividing for Traffic Safety," *Traffic Quarterly* 11:3 (July).

———. 1974. *Traffic Circulation Planning for Communities*. Los Angeles: Gruen Assoc.

McCluskey, Jim. 1979. *Roadform and Townscape*. London: Reed International.

Moudon, Anne Vernez, ed. 1987. *Public Streets for Public Use*. New York: Van Nostrand Co.

Mumford, Lewis. 1954. "The Neighborhood and the Neighborhood Unit," *Town Planning Review* 24, 4 (January).

———. 1961. *The City in History: Its Origins, Its Transformations, and Its Prospects*. New York: Harcourt, Brace, Jovanovich.

National Housing Agency. Technical Series no. 1. 1947. *A Checklist for the Review of Local Subdivision Controls*. Washington, DC: NHA.

Organization of Economic Co-operation and Development. 1976. "Geometric Road Design Standards," in *Proceedings of the Organization of Economic Co-operation and Development*. Paris: OECD (May).

Partridge, Ballamy. 1952. *Fill 'er Up!—The Story of Fifty Years of Motoring.* Chicago: McGraw-Hill.

Perry, Clarence Arthur. 1939. *Housing for the Machine Age.* New York: Russell Sage Foundation.

Practical Street Construction. 1916. Reprints from *Municipal Journal.* New York: Municipal Journal and Engineer.

Proceedings of The Second National Conference on City Planning and the Problem of Congestion, May 1910, Rochester, New York. Cambridge, MA: Harvard University Press.

Reps, John. 1965. *The Making of Urban America: A History of City Planning in the United States.* Princeton, NJ: Princeton University Press.

Robinson, Charles Mulford. 1904. *Modern Civic Art; or, The City Made Beautiful.* New York: G. P. Putnam's Sons.

———. 1911. *The Width and Arrangement of Streets, A Study in Town Planning.* New York: The Engineering News Publishing Company.

Rowe, Peter G. 1991. *Making a Middle Landscape.* Cambridge, MA: The MIT Press.

Rudofsky, Bernard. 1969. *Streets for People.* New York: Anchor Press.

San Diego, City of. 1992. *Transit Oriented Development Design Guidelines.* San Diego, CA: Planning Department.

Sitte, Camillo. 1889, 1965. *City Planning According to Artistic Principles.* New York: Random House.

Sitwell, N. H. H. 1981. *Roman Roads of Europe.* New York: St. Martin's Press.

Solomon, Daniel. 1992. *ReBuilding.* New York: Princeton Architectural Press.

Southworth, Michael, and Eran Ben-Joseph. 1995. "Street Standards and the Shaping of Suburbia," *Journal of the American Planning Association* 61, 1: 65–81.

Southworth, Michael, and Peter Owens. 1993. "The Evolving Metropolis: Studies of Community, Neighborhood, and Street Form at the Urban Edge," *Journal of the American Planning Association* 59, 3: 271–288.

Speed Management Through Traffic Engineering. 1992. *Accident Analysis and Prevention* (Special Issue) 24, 1.

Stilgoe, John. 1988. *Borderland: Origins of the American Suburb 1820–1939.* New Haven, CT: Yale University Press.

Summerson, John. 1949. *John Nash: Architect to King George IV.* London: George Allen & Unwin.

———. 1962. *Georgian London: An Architectural Study.* New York: Praeger.

Temple, Nigel. 1979. *John Nash & The Village Picturesque.* Gloucester: Allan Sutton.

Tripp, Alker. 1938. *Road Traffic and Its Control.* London: Edward Arnold.

Tucson, City of. 1991. *Neighborhood Protection Technique and Traffic Control Study.* Tuscon, AZ: Department of Transportation.

United States Department of Agriculture, Office of Road Inquiry. 1895. *Road Building in the United States*, Bulletin No. 17. Washington, DC: Government Printing Office.

Untermann, Richard K. 1990. "Accommodating the Pedestrian: Adapting Towns and Neighborhoods for Walking and Bicycling," in *Personal Travel in the US, Volume II, A Report on Findings from the 1983–1984 Nationwide Personal Transportation Study*. Washington, DC: United States Department of Transportation.

———. 1987. "Design Standards for Streets and Roads," in *Public Streets for Public Use*, Anne Vernez Moudon, ed. New York: Van Nostrand.

Warner, Sam Bass. 1978. *Streetcar Suburbs: The Process of Growth in Boston, 1870–1900*, 2d ed. Cambridge, MA: Harvard University Press.

Weiss Marc. 1987. *The Rise of the Community Builders*. New York: Columbia University Press.

Whyte, William H. 1964. *Cluster Development*. New York: American Conservation Association.

———. 1988. *City: An In-depth Look at the People, the Movement, and the Buildings that Make a City Live*. New York: Doubleday.

Wilson, William H. 1989. *The City Beautiful Movement*. Baltimore: Johns Hopkins University Press.

Wixom, Charles W. 1975. *Pictorial History of Road Building*. Washington, DC: American Road Builders' Association.

Wright, Henry. 1935. *Rehousing Urban America*. New York: Columbia University Press.

Index

ABOUT THE AUTHORS

Michael Southworth, Ph.D., FAIA, is Chair of the Department of City and Regional Planning and Professor in the Department of Landscape Architecture at the University of California at Berkeley. His work has included studies of the form of the evolving metropolis; reuse and preservation plans for older cities, neighborhoods, and buildings; and design of information systems to enhance the education and communication functions of cities. His books include *Maps: A Visual Survey and Design Guide, Ornamental Ironwork: An Illustrated Guide to Its Design, History, and Use in American Architecture*, and *A.I.A. Guide to Boston* (with Susan Southworth).

Eran Ben-Joseph, Ph.D., ASLA, is a Professor of Landscape Architecture and Planning at Virginia Polytechnic Institute and State University. He has worked as an environmental planner and landscape architect in Japan, Israel, and the United States. His work has included the design and planning of a ward in Tama New Town in Japan, urban renewal projects in Tokyo, and new communities in Israel. As a partner in the planning firm BNBJ in Tel Aviv he has designed and implemented many new forms of residential and urban streets, including the shared street concept. He is currently working on a book dealing with the aesthetic principles of traditional Japanese open spaces.